TODAY'S ISSUES 2

Adapted for youth from the best-selling
FACING THE ISSUES series

WILLIAM J. KRUTZA
AND PHILIP P. DI CICCO

Contemporary
Discussion Series

Baker Book House
Grand Rapids, Michigan 49506

Your World – Welcome to It!

FACING THE ISSUES — that's exactly what many youth say adults aren't doing. For some dissidents, everything is wrong with the world, and it's all the fault of those over thirty. Suddenly the world has gone all in the wrong direction. It either has to be changed or destroyed. Unfortunately, the destroyers seem to be getting more publicity than the changers. Of course, it's easier to bomb a building than change the attitudes of the people who work inside. It's easier to destroy a university than help it become a strong force for constructive change in society. Destruction is immediate; change takes time. Unfortunately, too many youth don't like to wait.

Christian youth are caught between the stability of their church life and the changeability of the issues of society. Because the church doesn't dive into every issue, some feel the church isn't saying enough about what's going on. If you're of that breed, remember that you are a part of the church. You are criticizing yourself as well as others. Is that what you really want to say — "I'm at fault?" If not, what are your constructive, life-changing, absolutely certain answers to all the issues of our society? And why haven't you given these answers to the world? Really, how many issues do you talk about with sufficient meaning to bring about answers? Make a list of all the issues you really haven't solved. Quite a list, isn't it?

That's what this book is all about — facing issues from a youthful point of view. The twelve issues in this book aren't all the issues in the world, by far. But it's a good start. Most likely there are issues here that you've never discussed before. And if you have, you probably haven't come up with one really earth-shaking solution. Join the crowd — it's your world. Welcome to it!

Why discuss issues? Basically because issues demand answers. We give an answer even when we say nothing about a problem. Silence can be one answer. But it's not usually youth's answer. And we'd rather you take the coffee-house approach — everyone speak up. Our fast-paced world constantly presents new areas of living that demand the development and application of moral and scriptural guidelines. Almost every week something new crops up — and if you as an under-thirty person are going to answer the world's great problems, you'd better keep busy tackling some of the everyday variety.

Possibly you've given a lot of superficial answers to the weighty issues of our society. Youth have a tendency to give stock answers, especially when they can blame adults for the mess we are in. As you delve into this book you'll find that blaming anyone isn't the answer we need, nor will you be able to come up with one-sentence answers. You'll enter into an exciting approach to life — not only identifying problems, but brainstorming to find Christian answers.

Who doesn't have *problems!* It's *answers* we need. And since it takes so few years to make an adult out of you, you'll soon be in the position where others will be looking at you as either the cause or the cure of the world's ills. Enter the door of discussion with others in your group and you'll be on the road to providing some answers.

This book isn't designed to give you the answers to the issues. Its purpose is to state the case from a variety of viewpoints and then let you come up with the answer that best fits your situation. Pay particular attention to the "What Does the Bible Say?" sections. The Bible doesn't come out with dogmatic statements of conduct in every case, but it does provide those principles which can answer the knotty problems of today. If the Bible is absolutely clear on a subject, there's no issue about it. You will have to dig into the Scriptures even beyond the verses listed from the two modern versions to find fully satisfying answers. Don't neglect this important part of your preparation for the discussion. The Bible will provide those timeless principles that will help you establish the best approaches to your world.

It really is your world. The issues are yours to face. What will your answers be? By honest searching and open discussion of the issues in this book, it is hoped that you will be better prepared to live in your world. Then you'll be more eager to tell others, "Welcome to it!"

Contents

Population Explosion — Should Christians Care? 1

NONE OF US LIKES TO THINK OF OURSELVES as "one too many." It's nice to feel that we have an important place to fill on this planet, and we would like to stay on it a long time. We shudder to think that some of us might not have made it if our parents had limited their offspring to two children. Yet population experts are strongly suggesting this as one answer to the accelerating population growth. The problem of the growing population is a serious one — especially for young people who'll have to live on an overpopulated earth.

Population experts have been warning us that runaway population growth will guarantee our extinction. The population explosion "carries all the elements of catastrophe, famine, plague and major war." The *Manchester Guardian* warned, "The future is doom-laden so long as we shrink from tackling the true runaway element in the world scene: the population explosion. Within the next generation or two the world population will have to be stablized if there is not to be global catastrophe."

Dr. Paul R. Ehrlich, professor of biology at Stanford University, and a specialist on population, paints a gloomy picture, saying that the battle to feed humanity is lost. He predicts famine in the 70s for millions of people in spite of crash programs aimed at preventing it. The most that can be done now, according to Ehrlich, is to "stretch" for a time the capacity of the earth to provide food by increasing food production. The only hope is a worldwide effort by all nations to control population. Ehrlich says, "Population control is the conscious regulation of the number of human beings to meet the needs, not just of individual families, but of society as a whole."

A dwindling food supply, pollution of the environment, the battle against disease and the psychological effects of overcrowding are all problems that stem from having too many people. While pure technology can solve some of these problems for a time, the only effective solution seems to be rigid population control programs.

Population experts are concerned with the percentage of growth. Even a small increase presents enormous problems. It has been estimated that in 8000 B.C. there were about five million people on the earth. When Christ walked the earth there were about three hundred million people. During that eight-thousand-year period the world population doubled six times. On an average, it had taken more than a thousand years for the population to increase twofold.

Between 1650 and 1815 population information became more accurate. During these 165 years the population not only doubled, but surpassed the one billion mark. By 1920, 105 years later, the population doubled again. Around

1975 the population is expected to double again — after only 55 years — to about four billion people. By the mid 1980s there will be five billion people on the earth. Before the end of the century, there will be seven billion people seeking food and shelter.

Underdeveloped countries will suffer most from the population explosion in the coming years. While the developed countries have sophisticated farm technologies that produce enormous amounts of food per acre, underdeveloped countries are still hundreds of years behind in both agricultural methods and production. Because of the complex problems of distribution, economics and politics, the richer nations cannot be expected to supply enough food.

However, rich nations can offer technology and ability to help poorer countries change political and religious prejudices that are root causes of the problem. Poor nations make up about two-thirds of the world's population, but have only one-sixth of the world's income. Over a billion people have an income of only $100 to $250 *per year*. A little less than one billion live on incomes under $100. Some countries average less than that — Burma, $65; India, $90; Haiti, $70. Uneven distribution of wealth adds to the problem. In Columbia, 60 percent of the nation's income is controlled by 20 percent of the people, and over two-thirds of the agricultural land is owned by a 4 percent minority of rich landowners.

These gaps between the rich and the poor both within nations and between nations threaten the whole human race. Tensions brought about by these disparities add more unrest and create greater disharmony between people. The rich must help the poor and the poor must want to be helped. Crash programs by the developed nations to aid their underdeveloped neighbors must include education, training in literacy, and information on population control methods. The recipients, in turn, must voluntarily accept birth control or potential gains from such aid would only be swallowed up by the swelling masses of people. Rich nations must have no ulterior motives in giving aid. The survival of the human race is at stake.

There is hope that the United States can achieve a "zero population growth" of about 275 million. Pressures from environmentalists and the economics of life are contributing factors. If this comes true it would mean there would be less need for schools, more women would work outside the home and more stability in planning for economic growth could be achieved because no single age group would dominate the population. The census bureau shows that if the population were to stabilize sixty-five to seventy years from now at about 275 million, that age groups from one to ten, ten to twenty, twenty to thirty, etc., would stabilize at around 35 to 37 million per group.

Christians have a mandate from God to "subdue" the earth. This speaks of a control over nature, which includes controlling the human population. The Bible emphasizes the quality of human life and Christians have responsibilities to maintain high standards. We are now aware that the possibility of decreasing our chances of giving more people a "good life" is threatened more than ever by expanding populations.

One practical way to solve this problem is to limit families to two children or less in order to achieve a zero population growth. Dr. Paul Ehrlich says the first thing we can do to reduce population is to "set an example [and] don't have more than two children." One writer has gone so far as to say that to have more than two children is a "crime far worse than larceny."

The Catholic Church up to this point has opposed population control measures. Pope Paul VI shocked Catholics and Protestants when he reaffirmed the Catholic Church's stand against birth control. In practice, however, many Catholics do not follow the official church stand. Most Protestants support family planning and birth control programs.

Christians must tackle the population problem and seek biblical guidance. Young people preparing for marriage need to think through this problem and condition themselves to answer it. Population control is more than a biological necessity or a moral issue, it is a spiritual concern for Christian young people.

Christian young people are growing up in an era that imposes many changes on them. Perhaps the government will restrict the number of children or tax an excess of two. There will be new methods of birth control. Social pressures will be put upon larger families. There might even be discrimination against large families.

13

Christians will have to rethink some of their present attitudes. The population problem can only be solved if everyone upon the earth is concerned. Those who desire more children must think of their children's future.

Christian young people can do their part by carefully planning for their future and by considering the consequences of the growing population. For those who want to and can afford to have more than two children there is always the possibility of adoption, a growing practice among those concerned about the quality of life and the future of our planet.

WHAT DOES THE BIBLE SAY?

"God blessed them; God said to them: Be fruitful; multiply; fill the earth and subdue it; bear rule over the fish of the sea; over the birds of the air and over every living, moving creature on earth" (Gen. 1:28).

"God also remembered Rachel; God heard her and rendered her fertile. She conceived and gave birth to a son; she said, 'God has removed my reproach'" (Gen. 30:22-23).

"But to Hannah he gave a double portion; for he loved Hannah although the Lord had closed her womb. Her rival, however, provoked her mercilessly to make her irritable, because the Lord had closed her womb" (I Sam. 1:5-6).

"And seven women will grasp one man in that day, saying, 'We will eat our own bread, and we will wear our own clothes;

only let us be called by your name; take away our stigma' " (Isa. 4:1).

"Behold, children are a legacy from the Lord; the fruit of the womb is His reward. As arrows in the hand of a mighty man, so are the children of one's youth. Blessed is the man who has his quiver full of them" (Ps. 127:3-5).

"The greatest in the Kingdom of heaven is the one who humbles himself and becomes like this child. And the person who welcomes in my name one such child as this, welcomes me. As for these little ones who believe in me — it would be better for a man to have a large millstone tied around his neck and be drowned in the deep sea, than for him to cause one of them to turn away from me. How terrible for the world that there are things that make people turn away! Such things will always happen — but how terrible for the one who causes them! See that you don't despise any of these little ones. Their angels in heaven, I tell you, are always in the presence of my Father in heaven" (Matt. 18:4-7, 10).

WHAT DO YOU SAY?

1. Does the biblical command to "multiply" in Genesis 1:28 mean that Christians should ignore population control?

2. Should governments create laws to limit the size of families, or penalize (tax) large families? Would this be discrimination?

3. Many Christians oppose birth control. Is this a sensible attitude in the light of the dangers of overpopulation? Are there biblical reasons to oppose family planning?

4. Is the idea of limiting families contrary to the biblical idea of the blessing of many children (Ps. 127:3-5)?

5. What is the significance of the population explosion on evangelism? Should Christians limit themselves to evangelism and let others solve population and hunger problems?

6. Why might it be important to spend time feeding and training people before we begin our evangelism? Can it be done at the same time?

7. Should Christians support governmental programs to bring about a zero percentage rate in population growth? Why or why not?

8. Should the local church as a church take a stand on the population control issue? How? If not, why not? What can and should the church do to help young people in family planning?

9. Is having more than two children a moral issue in the light of overpopulation? Can birth control become a moral obligation?

10. What can young people do to encourage zero population growth? As a group? Personally? Can we expect poorer nations to accept population control without practicing some program of limiting our own population?

11. Would you condone mass sterilization or abortion as methods of birth control? Why or why not?

Should We Bend Our Moral Standards? 2

ONE TEEN-AGER TOLD HER PARENTS, "People just don't think that way anymore. The rules are different than when you were young. It's okay to get involved with a boy as long as you're in love. The rules have changed." Have you heard arguments like this from other young people? The moral standards for all society, for both young and old, have been changing. They are far different than the standards of our grandparents — our society is more permissive than a generation or two ago.

People's values have changed, their habits are different, their economic and social aspirations are higher. People have more money to do what they want. They can indulge themselves in more pleasures than past generations could. Television, movies, books and magazines all reflect this change in values. Modesty is no longer respected. Vulgarity, violence, nudity and four-letter words are sprinkled throughout the media until most people have come to accept them as normal expressions of real life. The volume and intensity of exposure to these things has revolutionized our customs and standards. Rather than fight, many people change their outlook to fit the popular mold. Christians, as a part of society, have been influenced by the new cultural "freedom" and have adopted new ways of looking at moral standards. One of the greatest tasks a young person faces today is that of determining how far to take this freedom. How much must be rejected as immoral? How and when should he change his moral values within a Christian context?

The new morality is not as restrictive as the old moral codes. The new morality claims to have a more honest approach to life than the puritanical rigidity upon which most of the older generation built its standards. Some young people believe that the old morality degenerated into a hypocritical double standard, which allowed adults to have one code of ethics for themselves and another for children and youth. They never took the old morality seriously because they saw much hypocrisy in the older generation — a "don't do as I do, do as I say" morality. The new morality is not tied to any absolute moral standard handed down from the past, but is based on relationships between people.

Some new concepts of morality, such as playboyism, do not have any qualms about stating their opposition to Christian morality and to any other moral standards that restrict the individual from indulging in unlimited pleasures. Yet, many thinkers do not consider the playboy philosophy a new morality. To them it's a sophisticated version of an old immorality. It differs considerably from the new morality and the situation ethics advocated by recent theologians.

John A. T. Robinson and Joseph Fletcher are

two theologians who have popularized the new morality. Joseph Fletcher, in his book, *Situation Ethics,* says that the one binding principle in Christian situation ethics is the law of love. All other laws, rules, ideals and norms are dependent upon and valid only if they serve love in a particular situation. Love takes priority over every situation. Situation ethics idolizes love. Love is the only norm. It is constant though all else changes. Everything is relative except love. Love is always good. Whatever is loving in any situation is good. Love justifies the means.

The new morality has served as a needed corrective to some distorted ideas about love and morality. The strength of the new morality might be considered its freedom to act apart from restrictive and narrow codes that have outlived their usefulness and have lost their meaning. Its stress on love brings in an element often lacking in strict authoritarian regulations which place more emphasis on punishment than on reformation.

Evangelical leaders deny that there is any biblical basis for the new morality. New morality theologians like to use hypothetical situations to make their point. They pose a difficult moral issue and seek to find a universal ethic that applies to it. But the question rises whether we can take extraordinary situations as a way for establishing standards. Such hypothetical situations, as being left with your sister after a nuclear war and being faced with the problem of repopulating the earth; or being a mother in a concentration camp and getting pregnant by another man in order to be returned to your family, are not the moral issues which we face in our daily lives. Situation ethics tries to prove the rule by the exception and this easily distorts what is generally considered right or wrong.

A man does not have to decide daily whether he may steal a loaf of bread to provide food for his family — though there might be a time when he would have to consider that possibility if no other choices were open to him. In general, a man would not steal because inwardly he knows it is wrong. Nor would he cheat or make false promises — he has deep convictions about fairness and honesty. Breaking the rules in an extraordinary circumstance does not necessarily become the basis for establishing a normal moral standard or ethical guideline. Normal behavioral patterns should not be confused by citing hypothetical situations.

The new morality distorts love's relationship to law by holding that the law has been done away with in order that love might become the universal law. It is difficult to substantiate this by Scripture. The Bible does not teach suspension of moral law in favor of love. It claims that love is the fulfilling of the law (Romans 13:8). Love sums up what the law is all about (Romans 13:9). Love does not replace the law; it identifies itself with it and becomes the primary motivation or force to make the law more effective. The new morality and situation ethics confuse the meaning of love because they fail adequately to define it. By making love a panacea for all moral action it has diluted it and made it more or less a license to do what might be expedient in a particular situation.

While the new morality has tried to give dimension to love and put it in its rightful place, it has unwittingly made love a slogan and a cliché. Young people say glibly, "Why can't I do it if I love him?" "It's all right as long as we 'love' one another." When modern man talks about love without tying it to biblical concepts he makes love mean whatever he wants. Love is not the benevolent attitude and action we show toward others, it is a personal means for justifying self-gratification. Love is no longer a compelling, motivating force inspired by a caring and loving God, but a vague and empty concept stripped of all its morally binding content.

The Bible has no quarrel with elevating love to its proper place in the Christian life. Neither would it oppose the primacy of love as the basis for establishing moral standards. The Bible, however, does not separate love from law as is done in the new morality. The old morality may have erred by stressing law over love, but the new morality falls into a greater trap by stressing a self-indulgent love that negates moral principles. The biblical view is a marriage between the concepts of love and law. One must be tempered by the other. There must be a recognition of a "law of love" that binds us to God's high moral standards, and at the same time keeps us from a morbid rigidity. Then a recognition of a "love of law" ties us to an unshakable standard. Biblical morality is a perfect union of law and love, which avoids the two extremes of license and legalism. Only by following a biblical morality will a young person experience the freedom of Christian love within a given situation. It is not the situation alone that determines a Christian's response to a moral question; rather it is the Christian's response to God's love and God's law within the situation.

WHAT DOES THE BIBLE SAY?

"Woe to those who call evil good and good evil; who place darkness as light and light as darkness; who put bitter for sweet and sweet for bitter!" (Isa. 5:20).

"Do not think that I have come to do away with the Law of Moses and the teaching of the prophets. I have not come to do away with them, but to give them real meaning" (Matt. 5:17).

"You have heard that it was said, 'Do not commit adultery.' But now I tell you: anyone who looks at a woman and wants to possess her is guilty of committing adultery with her in his heart" (Matt. 5:27-28).

"Not long afterward Jesus was walking through the wheat fields on a Sabbath day. His disciples were hungry, so they began to pick heads of wheat and eat the grain. When the Pharisees saw this, they said to Jesus, 'Look, it is against our Law for your disciples to do this on the Sabbath!' Jesus answered: 'Have you never read what David did that time when he and his men were hungry? He went into the house of God and he and his men ate the bread offered to God, even though it was against the Law for them to eat that bread — only the priests were allowed to eat it' " (Matt. 12:1-4).

"And Jesus continued: 'You have a clever way of rejecting God's law in order to uphold your own teaching' " (Mark 7:9; see Mark 7:1-13).

"If you love me, you will obey my commandments. . . . Whoever loves me will obey my message" (John 14:15, 23).

"If you obey my commands, you will remain in my love, in the same way that I have obeyed my Father's commands and remain in his love. . . . This is my commandment: love one another, just as I love you. . . . And you are my friends, if you do what I command" (John 15:10, 12, 14).

"Be in debt to no one — the only debt you should have is to love one another. Whoever loves his fellow man has obeyed the Law. The commandments, 'Do not commit adultery; do not murder; do not steal; do not covet' — all these, and any others beside, are summed up in the one command, 'Love your neighbor as yourself.' Whoever loves his neighbor will never do him wrong. To love, then, is to obey the whole Law" (Rom. 13:8-10).

"And to all these add love, which binds all things together in perfect unity. Everything you do or say, then, should be done in the name of the Lord Jesus, as you give thanks through him to God the Father" (Col. 3:14, 17).

"The purpose of this order is to arouse the love that comes from a pure heart, a clear conscience, and a genuine faith. Some men have turned away from these and have lost their way in foolish discussions. They want to be teachers of God's law, but they do not understand their own words or the matters about which they speak with so much confidence. We know that the Law is good, if it is used as it should be used" (I Tim. 1:5-8; cf. vs. 9-10).

"If we obey God's commands, then we are sure that we know him. If someone says, 'I do know him,' but does not obey his commands, such a person is a liar and there is no truth in him" (I John 2:3-4).

"This love I speak of means that we must live in obedience to God's commands. The command, as you have heard from the beginning, is this: you must all live in love" (II John 6).

WHAT DO YOU SAY?

1. What attracts young people to the new morality? How does the new morality differ from traditional morality?

2. What is legalism and how can it be applied to the old morality? Is a morality based

on the Bible a legalistic ethic? What is the difference between legalism and Christian standards of morality?

3. Are there elements in the new morality that can have value for the Christian? If so, what are they?

4. Does the new morality assume that people are capable of doing good and right? Does it take into account the sinful condition of man?

5. How does traditional morality view love? What place does the Bible put on love as it relates to moral conduct?

6. Are there any "absolute" rules? Does an ethical principle or law become absolute if revealed by God? Is an absolute code of morals necessarily rigid or fixed? Explain. Are the Ten Commandments absolute laws?

7. Does the Bible speak of moral behavior in terms of "situations"? If so, in what sense? Give examples. How do circumstances affect ethical decisions?

8. Is bending or changing one's standards because of a particular situation always contrary to an absolute ethic? When wouldn't it be?

9. How can the new morality become an excuse for loose behavior? Give examples. Are these valid arguments against the new morality?

10. Why is the use of bizarre hypothetical situations a poor basis for establishing one's moral standards? Should the exception ever determine the rule of moral standards?

11. Does a code, such as the Ten Commandments, offer a more stable moral structure than a moral system built apart from fixed standards?

How? Describe how we can base our moral standards on the Ten Commandments.

12. If the principles of the new morality were carried out to their logical conclusions, would civil law survive? What kind of society would develop?

Is Pollution a Christian Concern? 3

WHEN OIL SLICKS DEVELOPED off the coast of California, young people were the first on the scene trying to save the wildlife and reduce damage to the beach areas. These young people did not take a *ho hum* attitude toward the problem of man's environment.

Those who would like to spend another fifty or sixty years on this planet show an intense concern about what is happening to the air we breathe, the water we drink and the land we enjoy. Young people recognize that man has taxed nature to the point that it is fast becoming sterile and polluted and may no longer be able to produce the benefits we now take for granted. Americans must be concerned about their land today if they want to avoid a vast wasteland tomorrow. Christian young people should be vitally concerned also because, like others, they put part of the strain on our environment.

In his lifetime, an American will put about fifty times more of a burden on the environment than a person in India. With only 6 percent of the world's population, the United States consumes 40 percent of the earth's production of natural resources. In his lifetime, an American uses twenty-six million gallons of water, ten

27

thousand pounds of meat, twenty-eight thousand pounds of milk, twenty-one thousand gallons of gasoline, and over $21,000 worth of school buildings, clothing and furniture.

Our staggering production and consumption is not only a giant testimony to our affluence, but also a measure of our filth. We are running out of places to put our waste. In a year's time Americans junk seven million automobiles, one hundred million tires, twenty million tons of paper, twenty-eight billion bottles, and forty eight million cans. Garbage collection costs $2.8 billion a year. It is time to be alarmed when a nation produces 50 percent of the world's industrial pollution, dumps 165 million tons of solid waste, and puts 172 million tons of smoke and fumes into the atmosphere.

Americans, of course, are not the only polluters. Our planet itself is at stake. This "spaceship earth" may become a haunted island in the universe. Primitive man, threatened by his environment, groped like an animal in caves and huts, but modern man faces a threat to his very existence — a threat which he caused himself.

Christian young people should be concerned about polluting the environment because they believe that God is the Author of all things. Christians feel a responsibility to the creation and to their Creator. Christian concern comes out of obedience to the biblical mandate to "replenish" the earth. Yet some non-Christians accuse Christianity of contributing to our present ecological problems. They support their argument by saying that one of the basic teachings of both the Jewish and Christian faiths is that God intended plants, animals, birds and fishes for man's benefit. All things were created to serve man's purposes. Since Christianity paved the way for modern technology, it bears a burden of guilt for ecological chaos. Man's environmental problems arise from the fulfillment of the Christian teaching of man's dominance and transcendence over nature. These thinkers believe that since Christianity got us into our mess we need a new kind of religion to get us out. Unfortunately they do not recommend the true biblical answer.

Christians, however, are concerned about the environmental crisis and are willing to examine their approach. So-called Christian cultures are by no means the only ones which can be accused of exploiting the earth. The great early civilizations — Babylonia, Sumeria, Assyria, China, India and perhaps the Mayan civilization — overexploited the basic resources of the land. None of these had any relation to the Hebrew or Christian outlook.

No Christian can justify indifference toward the exploitation of nature. Christ frees a man from his natural self-centeredness and gives man a concern for others. Out of this concern for others, Christians become concerned about protecting the environment from those who would exploit it. Concerned Christians become interested in preserving the earth's resources because their attitudes are grounded in a firm belief in the value of everything created by God. Those who have no faith in a Creator, but who believe everything came by accident, would seem to be more likely the ones to be suspected of polluting and exploiting the earth as a result of their basic attitudes.

Rather than religion being the culprit for our environmental ills, perhaps the fault is due to lack of faith in the Creator who commissioned mankind to protect and preserve the earth. In fact, it was the repudiation of the biblical doctrine of creation by philosophers and scholars in the eighteenth and nineteenth centuries that has led to a nontheistic, nonscriptural concept of the universe. Since the earth "just happened," and was propelled by some unknown, random atoms colliding and cohering in an accidental manner, why should the environment be important?

With this view, it is easy for a young person to say, Why should I be concerned about the environment? It is merely a resource from which I can gain comforts, services and enjoyments. Why can't I exploit the ground, the water or the air for any advantage I choose? Isn't this progress? The earth belongs to *me*. It is *mine* to use.

This attitude is at the root of our present pollution crisis. Men have ignored the biblical mandate to care for the earth which they occupy. Pollution is not caused because of Christian assumptions about the earth, though some Christians may have adopted bad habits that contribute to our polluted environment.

The Bible offers an adequate theology of ecology, but modern man has ignored what the Bible says. He has been too busy building new housing, skyscrapers and factories and other monuments to progress that pollute.

The biblical view of the environment is not based on exploiting natural resources, but on responsible stewardship. Christians should be among the most qualified to pave the way for setting ethical guidelines to help solve environmental problems. Biblical themes such as the creation story speak not only of dominion, but also of *responsibility, stewardship* and *respect* for nature. The earth belongs ultimately to God — "The earth is the Lord's and the fulness thereof" — but man is a trustee of nature. The Old Testament even speaks of "sabbatical" years — times when the fields would lie fallow to restore themselves. The wonder and majesty of nature are constant themes of the Psalms and the poetic literature of the Old Testament. Jesus reminds us that God takes notice of the falling sparrow and the lilies of the field.

Christian youth who study their Bibles will find enough precedent to take positive action in today's world to help solve the environmental crisis. There is much for young people to learn about the Christian stewardship of the earth. Sunday school discussion can surely get down to practical applications of biblical principles to the pollution problem.

How we dispose of our garbage, how we plan our cities, our methods of conservation, how we use the skies, the sea and land are all valid areas in which Christians may apply their faith in practical ways. Christian young people as well as adults must develop new attitudes and values if our environment is to be saved. We must learn to discipline ourselves to reduce the strain on our environment. We should emphasize new concern, stricter discipline, and conservation and thrift in the stewardship of our material resources. It is time that we replace our mania for pleasure, comfort, indulgence and luxury with a new moderation that balances our requirement for enjoyable life upon the earth against our need to tap its resources.

Pollution is a people problem. Christian young people can make a significant contribution to the future of society by taking an active and intelligent part in changing our attitudes toward our resources and our environment. The motive has to be greater than selfish interest in order to preserve the earth a little longer for those being born. Young and old need a firm belief that God's earth is beautiful and that we as His children have responsibilities for sustaining it.

Perhaps we should look at it in one other way. How can adults take youth seriously about the matters regarding which they express concern if they do not show a genuine concern about the future of their environment? Young people are just as much responsible for the future as their parents are and now is the time to prepare for making that future a fruitful one. Perhaps your children will take you more seriously about spiritual matters if they can see that you cared about your world when you were young. If you have been a good steward of that which is physical, they will assume you also are deeply concerned about the spiritual environment that you proclaim in Christ.

WHAT DOES THE BIBLE SAY?

"Then God said: Let Us make man in Our image, after Our likeness, and let them bear rule over the fish in the sea, over the birds of the air, over the animals; over the whole earth and over all creeping things that crawl on the earth. God blessed them; God said to them: Be fruitful; multiply; fill the earth and subdue it; bear rule over the fish of the sea; over the birds of the air and over every living, moving creature on earth. God saw that everything He had made was excellent, indeed" (Gen. 1:26, 28, 31).

"The Lord God took the man and placed him in the garden of Eden to cultivate it and to care for it" (Gen. 2:15).

"Speak to the Israelites, and tell them: When you come into the land which I give you, then the land shall have a Sabbath rest to the Lord. Six years you will sow your acreage; six years you will prune your vineyard and gather in the produce, but in the seventh year there shall be a restful Sabbath for the land, a rest toward the Lord: you shall neither sow your field nor prune your vineyard" (Lev. 25:2-4).

"Then I brought you into a garden land to eat of its fruit and its good things; but when you went in, you defiled My land

and made My inheritance an abomination"
(Jer. 2:7).

"The earth and all its fulness are the Lord's,
the world and all who live in it" (Ps. 24:1).

"Cast your bread upon the waters, for you
will find it after many days" (Eccles. 11:
1).

"Do not deceive yourselves: no one makes
a fool of God. A man will reap exactly
what he plants" (Gal. 6:7).

"Do not save riches here on earth, where
moths and rust destroy, and robbers break
in and steal. Instead, save riches in heaven,
where moths and rust cannot destroy, and
robbers cannot break in and steal" (Matt.
6:19-20).

"The first angel blew his trumpet. Hail and
fire, mixed with blood, came pouring down
on the earth. A third of the earth was
burned up, and a third of the trees were
burned up, and every blade of green grass
was burned up.
"Then the second angel blew his trumpet.
Something that looked like a large moun-
tain burning with fire was thrown into the
sea. A third of the sea was turned into
blood, and a third of all living creatures in
the sea died, and a third of all ships were
destroyed.
"Then the third angel blew his trumpet. A
large star, burning, like a torch, dropped
from the sky and fell on a third of the

rivers, and on the springs of water. (The name of the star is Bitterness.) A third of the water turned bitter, and many men died from drinking the water, because it had turned bitter" (Rev. 8:7-11).

WHAT DO YOU SAY?

1. Do you believe the accusation by non-Christians that the Christian-Jewish view of the world is a chief cause of our pollution problem? In what sense may it be valid? In what sense is it not?

2. What does Genesis 1:26-28 mean? Does it give man the right to exploit the earth? How do these verses speak against such exploitation?

3. Why should Christian youth take a serious part in helping solve environmental problems? Is it right for Christians to avoid getting involved in pollution control because it is not a "spiritual" problem? Why or why not?

4. In what ways has the church neglected the environmental problem? Is concern for the environment a legitimate concern for a local congregation?

5. In what sense is our environmental problem a moral one? Does the Christian view of sin come into play? How?

6. What should be the role of the church in the current crisis? Should the church use political leverage to help reduce pollution? How?

7. What practical things can a person do to help reduce air and water pollution? Should individuals be concerned or is the problem largely one for industry and government?

8. Are warnings against polluting the environment based on unwarranted fear? Is the danger overrated? Why has concern over pollution become an important issue? Wasn't it a problem fifty years ago?

9. Is it possible that the judgments spoken of in Revelation 8 are related to man's pollution of the earth?

10. Should Christians advocate reducing the birthrate to help slow down the depletion of natural resources? Is this contrary to Genesis 1:28?

11. Does a creationist provide a more consistent view of the world and the environment than one who makes naturalistic assumptions? Explain.

12. Will you do something about pollution if it means limiting and inconveniencing your pursuit of the good life? Will you drive your car less, keep it tuned, etc.? Will you voluntarily use less electricity and water?

13. Is modern man prepared for the austerity demanded to prevent a ravaged earth? Should there be government controls on people's habits?

Political Issues — Speak Up or Keep Silent? 4

IN A POLL OF SEVERAL THOUSAND YOUTH in February 1971, *Seventeen* magazine indicated that 55 percent of the youth considered themselves a part of the "silent majority." The survey revealed that 71 percent also considered their parents a part of that majority. From this we might conclude that young people are more concerned about political issues than their parents. But a recent *Life* survey showed that only 38 percent of the eighteen-year-olds indicated that they planned to vote in the next national election.

If you pay any attention to the mass media — especially to television — you can't avoid political issues. A few moments after the president of the United States or the premier of Canada make major decisions, these decisions are beamed across the country and around the world, and people are given the opportunity to form political judgments. Christian youth, like everyone else, are involved in political issues whether they choose to be or not. Even refusal to get involved puts a person in a political position — usually on that side which seeks to maintain the status quo. To say nothing is to join the silent majority.

In past decades, many believers considered that the church's active involvement in political affairs was contrary to our Lord's command to preach the gospel. They contended that if men's hearts were changed society would also change. Of course, this is only partially true – even if everyone became Christian, we would still need laws to govern interpersonal relationships.

Many Christians are now saying that we ought to get into the political arena. Christians should counteract political powers that perpetuate evils in our communities. Some Christian activists say that Christians should enter the political arena if only for the motive of self-preservation. Churches must become politically involved if for no other reason than to create or maintain a climate in which to be free to do its work.

A classic illustration of the church keeping silent in the face of losing its freedom occurred when Hitler rose to power in Germany. German pastors denounced Americans who criticized the silence of the German church. German youth, both non-Christian and Christian, made no protests against the despotism of Hitler. In fact, youth were a primary source of exploitation for his political power and military conquests.

Many parts of the church did not cry against slavery in the eighteenth and early nineteenth centuries. If Christians had opposed the slave trade with one voice, our civil rights struggles might have been eliminated years ago. Unfortunately, many Christians avoided the political involvement necessary to eliminate racial injustice.

The church has often entered the political arena and brought about great changes. During the early 1900s, the Anti-Saloon League, made up mostly of church people and supported mainly by church contributions, brought about the Prohibition Amendment. Much of this was accomplished by temperance clubs for young people.

Recently, in New York State, churches lobbied against proposed bingo legislation and against a proposed lottery for education. Although the churches lost, much church involvement was evident.

So you ask, What's the issue? Most young people believe in political involvement. While this may be true on an individual basis, even young people have to decide if political involvement should be a church matter.

As Malcolm Nygren, pastor of the First Presbyterian Church, Champaign, Illinois, says in reference to the Good Samaritan story, "He didn't make the road safe for travelers. . . . Political action would have been necessary for that." He, like many others, would support the idea that an individual Christian should show utmost concern for the needy and even get involved in seeing that their needs are met. But make it a church affair — never! He continues, "When the church tries to become a political leader, it harms both its own mission and the world it seeks to help."

The Reverend Nygren states that the church, though it has a tremendous ability to give moral direction on which political decisions can be made, has no special competence to offer in specific political decisions. Each member of a congregation should speak his own mind rather than give a corporate endorsement of a political view.

Take any particular political issue that is being discussed today. Poll the members of your Sunday school class or youth group as to their views. Immediately you'll notice a variety of opinions. You cannot speak for everyone in the group so you conclude that it's far better to let each person speak for himself. Many believe that the church should follow a similar policy when considering political issues.

If you think the church should speak corporately on a given political issue, you must answer some pertinent questions: Who should speak for the church? Who is qualified to give the church's political position? Would you delegate this task to the pastor? The chairman of the church board? Your Sunday school superintendent? Or do you want the task yourself? Should a consensus be reached by all the churches in a town or city? All the churches of one denomination?

Perhaps the church would provide a better service to society if it would define the moral principles involved in making political decisions. Perhaps this can be done through an open-minded pastor or through a concerned group of people in the church. This would help youth and adults face the issues and make practical decisions on the questions of individual involvement. By silence the church may commit a sin against its own members. To speak out on specific issues rather than defining the moral principles may rob individuals of making proper decisions in future situations.

Dr. Lewis Smedes, professor of religion and

theology at Calvin College, Grand Rapids, Michigan, says the church must speak on all issues that have moral dimensions. But he points out that the church must speak in terms of moral principles without invading the arena of political policy.

Though there is a lot of pessimism among young people as to the value of political involvement, the Christian young person must be optimistic. He must state and apply those biblical principles that govern man's relationships with other men. The Bible provides the best basis for moral principles to undergird worthwhile political pronouncements. And though the political process seems discouragingly slow, young people should not give up. They should enter the political arena with the goal of injecting Christian principles into the laws that govern society. They must determine in their own minds what God would have them say or do in the political arena and then say and do it courageously. Those principles which are learned as individuals in church will help young people face the world and help solve some of life's perplexing and demanding issues. Christian youth must make the all-important decision whether to speak up or to keep silent. Such a decision will determine the character of the church in the future.

WHAT DOES THE BIBLE SAY?

"Thus says the Lord: go down to the house of the king of Judah, and speak there this word, 'Hear the word of the Lord, O King

41

of Judah, who is sitting on the throne of David, you, your servants, and your people who enter these gates. Thus says the Lord: Execute right and justice. Deliver the plunderer out of the hand of the oppressor. Do neither wrong nor violence to the immigrant, the fatherless, or the widow; neither shed innocent blood in this place'" (Jer. 22:1-3).

"For to us a Child is born, to us a Son is given; the government shall be upon His shoulder; and His name shall be called Wonderful, Counselor, Mighty God, Everlasting Father, Prince of Peace. There shall be no end to the increase of [His] government" (Isa. 9:6-7).

"So Jesus said to them, 'Well, then, pay to the Emperor what belongs to him, and pay to God what belongs to God'" (Matt. 22: 21).

"Remind your people to submit to rulers and authorities, to obey them, to be ready to do every good thing" (Titus 3:1).

"Happy are those who work for peace among men: God will call them his sons!" (Matt. 5:9).

WHAT DO YOU SAY?

1. How do you determine which political issues are moral issues? Does a political issue have to become a moral issue before church people should become concerned about it?

2. What are some of the consequences of the church's past disinterest in political issues? Should the church make a distinction between spiritual and political areas of life? Why or why not?

3. What political issues should the youth of your church discuss? Should such discussion result in specific action?

4. Should the church openly support specific candidates in an election? What if an opposing candidate has views that could hurt the church's future?

5. Does a pastor have an obligation to preach on certain political issues? Who would determine which issues ought to be discussed? Would a discussion of these issues ever be more appropriate than a sermon? When and why?

6. If individual Christians have rights and obligations to become involved in political issues, should boards and committees within a church also have this privilege?

7. When Jesus said, "Render to the Emperor the things that are due to him, and to God the things that are due to God," was He advocating church-state separation or good citizen involvement? Explain.

8. Since Christians often disagree on political issues, is it right to judge a person's spirituality on the basis of his political views? How can this be avoided?

9. Is there any inconsistency in saying that individual Christians should be active in political issues and yet maintain that churches should not speak corporately on political issues?

10. What can be done to get more Christian

young people actively concerned about and involved in political affairs? Would greater Christian involvement have an influence on our society? Explain.

11. If you want to make a Christian impact on the political life of your community, state or nation, where would you start? How would you go about it?

Is TV Warping
Your Mind? 5

IF YOU'RE AN EIGHTEEN-YEAR-OLD, you've probably spent about fifteen thousand hours in front of a television set. And if you live to age sixty-five, you'll amass nine years of television viewing. If you go to Sunday school every week during your lifetime, you'll only get an equivalent of four solid months of Bible training. In other words, you'll spend about twenty-seven times as much time viewing TV as you will spend in learning the eternal truths of the Bible. No wonder some Christian leaders are concerned that Christian young people are having their minds and lives molded and possibly warped by TV.

Eliot Daley, writing in *TV Guide,* accuses TV of robbing children of their childhood. Children spend more time with the TV set than with their parents. They seldom see a complete family unit. They never see justice followed through by the due process of the law. Children have learned from TV that nothing takes time. Every problem is solved quickly and easily in an hour or less. Young people seem to have a heightened sense of outrage toward war, bigotry and pollution, but consider as useless all proposed solutions that do not solve the problems immediately. Because of the way TV handles most problems, some young people form naive attitudes toward solving problems. Then they face the problems of the real world, problems to which TV did not give the solutions.

Television is one of modern man's greatest inventions — especially when it is used for the purpose of mass education. Unfortunately, most of the time it is used simply to attract people to some commercial product. Manufacturers want to sell their products. That's why all the commercials. About 70 percent of children request items they have seen on TV, and about 80 percent of their parents give them their wishes. That's why manufacturers sponsor programs. That's why advertisers worry about program ratings.

It's unfortunate that the main entertainment media of the present generation is geared to selling products rather than to promoting both good entertainment and education.

In the case of low-income viewers, this is especially damaging because there is little means of obtaining in real life what is seen on TV.

No one can deny that TV teaches as well as entertains. In fact, it's possibly as good or better a teacher than most other audio-visual presentation. What TV teaches is something every Christian youth should analyze. Advertisers spend nearly $3 billion annually to change human behavior — to get viewers to switch brands. They use all kinds of appeals — many amoral, some immoral — to accomplish their purposes.

Arnold J. Toynbee, well-known historian and philosopher, says that viewers as well as producers share the blame for the type of available programming. If millions of people would stop watching a specific program, the network would soon drop the show and the sponsors would ask, Why? If Americans would only watch the superior programs, soon the mediocre and poor ones would be eliminated. Toynbee points out that the present low standards of programming are due to viewers' own choices. He says that we can't blame the producers. They seem to have sensed what the public wants. And to satisfy everyone, they pitch the programs somewhat below the mental norm of the listeners. Don't be fooled, the calculated mental age of the average viewer is less than that of a high school graduate.

Unfortunately, Toynbee observes, we won't change our childish TV tastes until we change our attitudes toward our leisure time. Too many Americans use leisure on what Toynbee calls "comparatively innocent frivolities." He warns that these will lead to social, cultural and moral regression if continued unchecked. And since TV reflects many social attitudes, we won't be able to expect much uplifting programming from the boob tube. If the "you get what you ask for" philosophy governs TV programming, then there's something dreadfully wrong in our society. Rather than being the peace-loving country we often like to imagine ourselves to be, our TV tastes expose our love for violence.

The National Commission on the Causes and Prevention of Violence reported in 1969 that the preponderance of available evidence strongly suggests that TV violence adversely affects viewers — especially youth and children. The child viewer is especially vulnerable because of his inability to distinguish between fantasy and reality. The constant image of violence as an accepted way of achieving ends and solving difficult situations can result in a distorted, pathological view of society.

Since the TV set is always accessible, in contrast to the limited availability of parents, it's no wonder that TV has so much influence upon children.

Albert Brandura, Stanford University psychologist, lists the following as some of the immediate effects of television and movie violence:

1. It reduces a viewer's inhibitions against violent, aggressive behavior,
2. It teaches viewers how to perform aggressive acts,
3. Even though the villain gets his deserts, the cure rarely erases the causes from the mind of the viewer.

Because TV presents so much violence, either by fact or fiction, we've accepted it as a normal reaction in society. We've become insensitive to human suffering through frequent exposure to antisocial behavior.

You probably ask why does TV present so much violence? Why can't programs be more educational and humorously entertaining? Sponsors are in the crowd-catching business. They need instant catching power if they are going to tempt viewers with their products. To catch a crowd, you need conflict. Several levels of conflict are available: debates, elections, strikes, games, fights, dangers, violence. The type of conflict that will deliver the largest crowd most efficiently is the conflict that gets the largest, most intense emotional response — physical violence. That's why we have so much violence on tv!

Television producers have also learned that news programs are one giant means of attracting an audience. And much news takes on violent aspects. In contrast to the fictionalized programs, news presents violence as fact! But the news also shows everything else either as it happens or shortly after. This doesn't allow the viewer much time to fit an instant event into a historical context. News programs also have the disadvantages of being able to present only highlights of the news. Viewers would not listen to an entire speech by the vice-president just to hear some particularly pungent remark. But broadcasting only that one remark, as is practiced by tv news programming, gives a distorted view of what was said. News highlights are always the dramatic aspects of life and tend to give the viewers a distorted view of life because most of life *is* mundane.

As a concerned Christian, you must also contend with the distorted, materialistic view of life presented on tv. You must analyze each program and review it according to your Christian principles. If programs need to be changed, you have to take the time and effort to challenge the producers of these distorted views of life.

Whenever possible, you should suggest biblical truths and principles that could be woven into programs. You might even accept the challenging task of becoming a tv producer, writer or performer, thus helping to present a morally balanced view of life.

49

". . . fill your minds with those things that are good and deserve praise: things that are true, noble, right, pure, lovely, and honorable" (Phil. 4:8).

"For surely you know this: when you surrender yourselves as slaves to obey someone, you are in fact the slaves of the master you obey — either of sin, which results in death, or of obedience, which results in being put right with God" (Rom. 6:16).

"So I find that this law is at work: when I want to do what is good, what is evil is the only choice I have. My inner being delights in the law of God. But I see a different law at work in my body — a law that fights against the law that my mind approves of. It makes me a prisoner to the law of sin which is at work in my body. What an unhappy man I am! Who will rescue me from this body that is taking me to death? Thanks be to God, through our Lord Jesus Christ!" (Rom. 7:21-25).

"Eat not the bread of him whose eye is selfish, neither desire his delicacies; for as one who inwardly figures the cost, so is he; 'Eat and drink,' he says to you, but his heart is not with you" (Prov. 23:6-7).

". . . as his followers you were taught the truth which is in Jesus. So get rid of your old self, which made you live as you used to — the old self which was being destroyed by its deceitful desires. Your hearts and minds must be made completely new. You must put on the new self, which is created in God's likeness, and reveals itself in the true life that is upright and holy" (Eph. 4: 21-24).

"Do not love the world or anything that belongs to the world. If you love the world, you do not have the love for the Father in you. Everything that belongs to the world — what the sinful self desires, what people see and want, and everything in this world that people are so proud of — none of this comes from the Father; it all comes from the world" (I John 2:15-16).

"As for these little ones who believe in me — it would be better for a man to have a large millstone tied around his neck and be drowned in the deep sea, than for him to cause one of them to turn away from me. How terrible for the world that there are things that make people turn away! Such things will always happen — but how terrible for the one who causes them!" (Matt. 18:6-7).

WHAT DO YOU SAY?

1. What standards of living are presented on TV? Do these promote a proper and realistic attitude toward life?

2. What views of life do you get from most TV programs? Would you adopt these views of life as your own? Why or why not? Do TV pro-

grams accurately reflect the American culture?

3. Do TV producers give the public the types of programs the public wants? If so, what does this reveal about the moral climate in our nation?

4. Name some of the good qualities of television. What does TV do best? What does it do worst? What is its chief value?

5. If you don't like a particular program, what can you do about it?

6. Much TV deliberately exploits violence for profit. Can this be changed? How? Does the portrayal of violence and sex on TV have an effect on viewers?

7. How can the public be educated to view more educational TV? What educational TV program in your area can you recommend?

8. Can the public be educated to demand better programming from the networks? How can people be educated apart from TV programs? How can people influence the networks?

9. Why should parents maintain surveillance of children's and youth programs? How can parents counterbalance the distorted and violent views of life presented on many programs?

10. What can Christians do to get programs on TV that could influence viewers toward Christ? How can your church get involved in producing and airing such programs?

Do You Really Care About Human Rights? 6

IN RECENT YEARS, we've heard many people talk about civil rights and human rights. Young people have been concerned about these rights, even demonstrating about them. The conflict over civil and human rights has often centered around the fear that by giving these rights to everyone some people would lose their own rights to private property and to privacy.

Wars have been fought to protect these basic rights. Yet we still seem to struggle to define their meaning and find effective ways to apply them to all people in our culture. In many instances, young people have proclaimed these rights as high ideals but have failed to show how they can be applied practically. Minority groups have always felt the brunt of the majority's monopoly on enjoying human rights and civil rights.

One must never forget that only as the rights of minorities are protected are the rights of the majority assured.

Some Christians have maintained the majority's status quo by acting as if rights aren't a Christian concern. They assume that if people accept the gospel, the problems of human rights will automatically be solved. But this attitude is a denial of our Christian heritage. Christians in past centuries have always been in the forefront in protecting human rights. If these are to be maintained in the future, Christians must become actively concerned about human rights.

A basic principle must be clear: everyone, regardless of race or geographical location, is entitled to certain opportunities as a human being. Rights are what a man is entitled to, not what society is willing to let him have. Some of these rights are: the right to choose one's own religion; the right to choose a political party; the right to think as one pleases; the right to assemble with others.

The United Nations adopted a Universal Declaration of Human Rights in 1948. Among those included are these important rights:

Article 1. All human beings are born free and equal in dignity and rights. They are endowed with reason and conscience and should act towards one another in a spirit of brotherhood.

Article 3. Everyone has the right to life, liberty and security of person.

Article 12. No one shall be subjected to arbitrary interference with his privacy, family, home or correspondence — nor to attack upon his honor and reputation. Everyone has the right to the protection of the law against such interference or attack.

Article 18. Everyone has the right to freedom of thought, conscience and religion; this right includes freedom to change his religion or belief, and freedom, either alone or in community with others and in public or private, to manifest his religion or belief in teaching, practice, worship and observation.

Article 19. Everyone has the right to freedom of opinion and expression; this right includes freedom to hold opinions without interference and to seek, receive and impart information and ideas through any media regardless of frontiers.

Former Attorney General of the United States, Ramsey Clark adds another right, that of privacy. He says that privacy is essential to the development of individual personality. The other great liberties are empty without it. Clark claims that privacy is the ultimate freedom. Only with privacy can we do what we desire. Only in privacy can we achieve the expressions of personal fulfillment toward others. The great Supreme Court justice Louis D. Brandeis spoke of privacy as "the right to be let alone, the most comprehensive of rights and the right most valued by civilized man."

We've heard considerable argument about the invasion of privacy by governmental law enforcement agencies. This can easily be done with electronic monitoring devices which have been held legal for obtaining information related to organized crime and national security. But Ramsey Clark believes that even in such cases, these devices are an illegal encroachment upon personal privacy.

Human rights such as freedom of expression are always limited in totalitarian countries. The Soviet Union and Communist China are prime examples. All writings must be censored. No creative writing is allowed in print that says anything against any governmental policy or program. In fact, the writer is in danger of extended imprisonment if he says anything contrary to government propaganda. Freedom has been reduced to the "privilege" of praising only the communist system.

Radicals in the United States who advocate the repression of some of our basic freedoms would not be able to express themselves in the Soviet Union. While by their campaigns against the establishment they abuse the freedom which allows them to express themselves in the United States, they are undermining the laws that guarantee their right to speak in a free society. Their abuses of these rights endanger not only their rights, but the rights of all citizens.

Concern for human rights is deeply rooted in Christian thinking. Jesus defines much of His mission in terms of liberation. He quoted Isaiah 61:1, 2 when He stated His mission of preaching the Good News to the poor, release for the captives, giving of sight to the blind, and providing liberty for the oppressed. Jesus constantly preached that Christians must be concerned about others. In Luke 18 we find this encouragement:

— the legal vindication of those wrongly accused, particularly widows;
— social acceptance of repentant outcasts;
— adult protection of all the rights of infants;
— a radical alleviation of poverty by the rich;
— the selection of special assistance for the hopelessly afflicted.

In paraphrasing Matthew 25:34-40, we see, 1) the rights of the hungry and the thirsty; 2) the rights of the refugee and the immigrant; 3) the rights of the poor and the naked; 4) the rights of the sick and the imprisoned; 5) the rights of the "least."

To follow in the footsteps of Christ, we must constantly be aware of the rights of others — those rights which are directly related to them as persons. The gospel presents the Christian as one prepared to forego his own rights and privileges to advance the rights of others.

Human rights must extend beyond the rhetoric that only blasts away at the ills of our society. If we are to counteract oppression in our world, we must do something to protect and promote the rights of others. Our neglect of positive action will promote the demise of our own rights.

How much are you really in favor of human rights? Are you really willing to let others have their rights if it means limiting your own? Are you prepared to have Blacks, Indians, Puerto Ricans and other minority groups live in your section of town or buy the house next door? Such are the acid tests of real concern for human rights. Do we pass them?

WHAT DOES THE BIBLE SAY?

> "You will be doing the right thing if you obey the law of the Kingdom, which is found in the scripture, 'Love your neighbor as yourself.' But if you treat people according to their outward appearance, you are guilty of sin, and the Law condemns you as a lawbreaker" (James 2:8-9).

> "As for you, my brothers, you were called to be free. But do not let this freedom be-

come an excuse for letting your physical desires rule you. Instead, let love make you serve one another. For the whole Law is summed up in one commandment: 'Love your neighbor as yourself.' But if you act like animals, hurting and harming each other, then watch out, or you will completely destroy one another" (Gal. 5:13-15). "Learn to do good! Seek justice; restrain the ruthless; protect the orphan; defend the widow" (Isa. 1:17).

"He has declared to you, O man, what is good, and what does the Lord require of you but to do justice, to love mercy and to walk humbly with your God?" (Micah 6:8).

"The Spirit of the Lord God is upon me; for the Lord has anointed me to preach good tidings to the humble; He has sent me to heal the brokenhearted; to proclaim liberty to the captives and the opening of the prison to those who are bound" (Isa. 61:1).

"Thus says the Lord: maintain justice and practice the right, for My salvation is close at hand and My victory is ready to be revealed" (Isa. 56:1).

"He sins who despises his neighbor, but happy is he who is gracious to the humble. . . . He who oppresses the poor insults his Maker, and he who is kind to the needy honors Him" (Prov. 14:21, 31).

"You have heard that it was said, 'An eye for an eye and a tooth for a tooth.' But now I tell you: do not take revenge on someone who does you wrong. If anyone slaps you on the right cheek, let him slap your left cheek too. . . . You have heard that it was said, 'Love your friends, hate your enemies.' But now I tell you: love your enemies, and pray for them who mistreat you, so that you will become the sons of your Father in heaven . . ." (Matt. 5:38-39, 43-45).

"Then the King will say to the people on his right: 'You who are blessed by my Father: come! Come and receive the kingdom which has been prepared for you ever since the creation of the world. I was hungry and you fed me, thirsty and you gave me drink; I was a stranger and you received me in your homes, naked and you clothed me; I was sick and you took care of me, in prison and you visited me.' The righteous will then answer him: 'When, Lord, did we ever see you hungry and feed you, or thirsty and give you drink? When did we ever see you a stranger and welcome you in our homes, or naked and clothe you? When did we ever see you sick or in prison, and visit you?' The King will answer back, 'I tell you, indeed, whenever you did this for one of these poorest brothers of mine, you did it for me!'" (Matt. 25:34-40).

WHAT DO YOU SAY?

1. What is the biblical basis for human rights?

Give some examples of the defense of human rights in the Bible. In what ways has the church promoted and protected these rights?

2. Why does society always seem to want to limit human rights rather than to expand them? Why do many nations refuse to recognize basic human rights?

3. Since our constitution guarantees certain rights, why haven't these rights been given to all our citizens? Why do some desire to maintain the status quo?

4. Do human rights change? If so, how? Does this make it difficult to help all citizens enjoy such rights?

5. Can true human rights be a lasting reality without accepting Christian teachings? Why or why not?

6. Soon a considerable amount of information about you will be stored in computers and may be available upon demand. How can you protect yourself from what might easily become an invasion of privacy? Or from computer errors?

7. How much should you as a Christian enter into the struggle with others in the preservation or gaining of human rights? Should Christians crusade for such rights?

8. Has the meaning of liberty and freedom been changed in the past couple decades? How? Do we have more or less freedom today? Why?

9. What is the difference between our understanding of human rights in America and the concept of human rights in the USSR? Why is there such a difference?

10. How have constitutional rights in America benefited the church? You as an individual?

minority groups? Is our present system under which these rights are protected worth protecting? What can and are you doing to see that human rights continue to be protected in this country?

Is War Ever Right? 7

FORMER PRESIDENT DWIGHT EISENHOWER, one of America's greatest generals, said, "I have come to hate war. War settles nothing." Thomas Jefferson said, "War is an instrument entirely inefficient toward redressing wrong." General Douglas MacArthur said of war that its "very destructiveness on both friend and foe has rendered it useless as a means of settling international disputes." Yet wars and threats of wars continue to plague the human race. In 1960 a Norwegian, using a computer, figured out that in 5,560 years of recorded history man has fought 14,531 wars (over 2½ per year) and in 185 generations mankind has had only ten years of peace!

Young people are especially concerned about war. When it comes down to it, very few people relish the idea of having to fight. Young people today have grown up in a world where war is a major social issue. War not only creates its own problems, but influences other segments of life, such as the economy, availability of funds for social welfare and alleviation of domestic problems such as pollution and education. Young people are sensitive about war — especially a difficult one like that in Vietnam, which is not a war of self-defense for America. The question of war, however, is broader than one war in a far-off country. Christians are concerned with the moral problems of war itself.

Christians have always had problems concerning the morality of war, but practical considerations and an attempt to face realistically the problems of aggression and exploitation have led to the concept of a "just" war. The idea of a "just" war was developed to account for the seeming contradiction of warfare and Christian love. Christians had to find some harmony be-between the biblical call to nonresistance and the moral right to defend one's person and possessions.

Christians have taken different approaches toward wars. Some maintain a pacifist position and oppose all wars. Mennonite and Quaker Christians are the best known pacifist groups. Others, including most evangelical Christians, hold to the just-war theory, which holds that if a war can be justified on the basis of protection of freedom it is all right to participate in such a war and support it. During World War II, Christians went to war against Hitler and Mussolini to preserve "freedom and justice" for all people. World War I might be considered a holy war. President Wilson's hope to make it the "war to end all wars" became a holy crusade to "make the world safe for democracy."

War is repugnant to most Christians. A hatred of violence and a quest for peace has convinced some Christians that war in itself is wrong. Therefore, to participate in it is unchristian. Pacifists base their arguments on two factors:

the teaching and example of Christ, and the effectiveness of nonresistance.

For the pacifist, war is contrary to God's will and inconsistent with faith in Christ. Jesus said that Christians should not resist evil (Matt. 5:39), and should love their enemies (Matt. 5:44). Pacifists believe these commands apply to nations as well as to individuals. Christ instructed His disciples never to meet personal hostility by striking back (Matt. 5:39; 26:52); rather they were to submit to it in order to overcome it by love. This method may not prove to be the most practical in terms of transforming evil men or nations, but pacifists maintain that Christians must be prepared to suffer even as Christ suffered.

Secondly, pacifists reason that since war has failed to reconcile men to each other, another alternative must be used to diminish hostility between nations. The causes of armed conflict often continue to exist after the conflict is over, and so-called "settlements" are usually based on the victor's force rather than on principles of justice. The injustices that remain, then, cause future wars. Victors often find "reasons" for expanding their power and become aggressors themselves (witness Soviet Russia's conquest and subjugation of Eastern Europe after World War II). War begets war. If war cannot persuade men toward peace, perhaps pacifism can. Peace begets peace.

One of the basic arguments against pacifism is that it does not consider the sinful nature of man. When nations wage war they are not only expressing political or national strategy for conquest, they are expressing greed and envy that stems from the condition of the human heart. War is evidence of man's pride expressed collectively as a national policy. Man's sinfulness is evidenced most hideously in following a policy of war that causes millions of people to die innocently and suffer unbearably. This produces hatred between men who otherwise would bargain, trade and live peacefully with each other.

Many Christians, then, feel that the sinfulness of man makes the position of the pacifist (who thinks pacifism will deter the aggressive forces of a warring nation) untenable. They feel that pacifism as an expression of individual conviction is one thing; but as a national policy, with so many people's lives at stake, it breaks down as an effective weapon against aggressive behavior. Christians must at times face the necessity of choosing between the lesser of two evils, simply because the sinful heart of man will not or cannot respond to reason or to love.

Any nation that refuses to defend its people and land against attack is abandoning its basic responsibility. The state exists to help maintain order and restrain those who choose to create chaos. Is it thinkable for a nation to adopt a "love your enemies" approach toward an aggressive, brutal and unprincipled foe? It would be unjust to refuse to defend one's self, one's friends and one's loved ones in such a situation. The only course is a "just" war.

Paul Ramsey, in his book *War and the Christian Conscience,* advocates a reassertion of the just-war concept as a fulfillment of the biblical command to love one's neighbor. He bases his idea on three points: (1) the just-war theory puts brotherly love in a wider political and social context — it is *not* a lowering of ethical standards; (2) the norm of conduct in such a war is the principle of Christian love; (3) Christians are not bound to absolute obedience to the state as citizens under God's rule. A *just war* is conceived of in terms of defense. Love is the motive. Wartime killing is "just" if it issues from a right intention (defense against aggression or oppression) and if the acts of killing are in proportion to the end in view.

Ramsey opposes total nuclear war because so many civilians are involved. The mass annihilation of mankind can never be considered "just." Strategic bombing of military installations is far different from immoral killing of civilian populations. Unlimited warfare, therefore, is never justifiable. The possibility of total nuclear war undercuts the idea of a just war. How can total annihilation ever be just?

Christians must recognize that all war is insanity, and that fighting a just war does not make warfare good. It is simply a recognition of a practical reality. When Christians think of a just war, they must view it in terms of its historical context. A just war refers to a war with limited ends, which applies limited means. The just-war doctrine recognizes that injustices exist as the order of mankind. Few nations who have waged war have done so with completely just or good motives. The just-war doctrine acknowledges this and provides a way to live with this reality. It recognizes that wars will happen among men and that nothing short of engaging in limited war can be right in certain situations.

Christians who follow the just-war theory avoid the one extreme of pacifism, which could lead to destruction and annihilation for those who are victimized, and the other extreme of making war a moral cause, which can turn a nation into a military state. To advocate a just-war policy is not to justify war as an answer to men's disagreements, but to realistically deal with man's belligerence and sinfulness. It recognizes that war is wrong, yet affirms the right of self-existence which at times demands that a person must fight to protect his family, his friends — and *even* his country.

Christian young people today have to face the issue of war, not by emotional or violent outbreaks against a war's insanity and inhumanity, but with a cool, rational, sincere, and realistic approach to a very human reality. Most of all, they must be "peacemakers" in the name of Christ.

WHAT DOES THE BIBLE SAY?

> "Where do all the fights and quarrels among you come from? They come from your passions, which are constantly fighting within your bodies. You want things, but you cannot have them, so you are ready to kill; you covet things, but you cannot get them, so you quarrel and fight. You do not have what you want because you do not ask God for it" (James 4:1-2).

> "Happy are those who work for peace

67

among men: God will call them his sons!"
(Matt. 5:9).

"You have heard that it was said, 'An eye
for an eye, and a tooth for a tooth.' But
now I tell you: do not take revenge on
someone who does you wrong. If anyone
slaps you on the right cheek, let him slap
your left cheek too. You have heard that
it was said, 'Love your friends, hate your
enemies.' But now I tell you: love your
enemies, and pray for those who mistreat
you" (Matt. 5:38-39, 43-44).

"Do not think that I have come to bring
peace to the world; no, I did not come to
bring peace, but a sword" (Matt. 10:34).

"You are going to hear the noise of battles
close by and the news of battles far away;
but, listen, do not be troubled. Such things
must happen, but they do not mean that
the end has come" (Matt. 24:6).

"Then Jesus said to him: 'Put your sword
back in its place, for all who take the
sword will die by the sword" (Matt. 26:
52).

"Glory to God in the highest heaven! And
peace on earth to men with whom he is
pleased!" (Luke 2:14).

"Come, see the works of the Lord! Who
brings desolations in the earth; Who makes
wars to cease to the ends of the earth; He
breaks the bow into pieces and snaps the

spear in two. He burns the chariots in the fire" (Ps. 46:8-9).

"For everything there is an appointed season, . . . a time to love, a time to hate; a time for war, and a time for peace" (Eccles. 3:1, 8).

"He shall arbitrate between the nations and shall decide [disputes] for many peoples; they shall beat their swords into plowshares and their spears into pruning shears; nation shall not lift up sword against nation, nor shall they learn war any more" (Isa. 2:4).

"You shall not murder" (Exod. 20:13).

"Now then, you go and strike down Amalek; destroy all he has; spare none, Slay man and woman, child and infant, cattle and sheep, camel and donkey" (I Sam. 15:3).

"Do everything possible, on your part, to live at peace with all men" (Rom. 12:18).

"Then I saw heaven open and there was a white horse. Its rider is called Faithful and True; it is with justice that he judges and fights his battles. His eyes were like a flame of fire, and he wore many crowns on his head. He had a name written on him, but no one except himself knows what it is. The robe he wore was covered with blood. The name by which he is called is 'The Word of God.' The armies of heaven followed him, riding on white horses and

dressed in clean white linen. A sharp
sword came out of his mouth, with which
he will defeat the nations. He will rule
over them with a rod of iron, and he will
squeeze out the wine in the winepress of
the furious wrath of the Almighty God. On
his robe and on his leg was written the
name: 'King of kings and Lord of lords'"
(Rev. 19:11-16).

WHAT DO YOU SAY?

1. What are some causes of war? What con-
stitutes a "war"? Is war inevitable? Why do
nations choose war to settle differences?

2. Define the meaning of a "just" war? What
war or wars can be considered to have been
just? Is the just-war concept Christian?

3. How does the just-war concept differ from
the pacifist view? Is there a biblical basis for
the just-war theory?

4. What is pacifism? Is it a scriptural concept? What are its strong points? What are its
weak points? What are the implications of Revelation 19:11-16 for Christian pacifists?

5. Do New Testament passages dealing with
nonviolence support the pacifist point of view?
Do these passages apply to individuals or to
nations?

6. How do you explain the attitudes and
actions of the children of Israel when they con-
quered the land of Canaan and the warfare
during the Kingdom Period? Does the history
of Israel justify war today?

7. What did Jesus mean when He said,

"Love your enemies"? How can this be expressed? Is it possible to love your enemies and kill them at the same time? Is there a contradiction between the Old Testament portrayal of war and New Testament affirmation of love, peace and nonviolence?

8. Is it ever morally right to let an aggressor or oppressor torment or kill a friend? Would you use violence to defend a relative or friend? How does this apply to nations? Is there a difference?

9. What is the difference between killing in a war under orders and intentional murder? Does killing other people in a war ever become murder? Explain.

10. Is conscientious objection a Christian concept? Is it right to be unwilling to fight for one's country while others may have to lose their lives to defend it?

11. Should Christians support the present arms buildup as a preventative measure against war? Is the arms race a deterrent to war? What are the dangers?

12. Can a military career be an authentic "calling" for a Christian young person? If so, in what sense?

What Does Money Mean to You? 8

AN OFTEN-EXPRESSED ATTITUDE OF today's youth goes like this: We're not hung up on money; money doesn't mean so much to us that we're going to become slaves to the Establishment to earn it; we can take it or leave it; we've finally matured to the place where we understand the meaning of money.

But is this really true? Don't most young people enjoy the things money can buy? Most manufacturers of consumer goods think so. Notice the TV ads. Many of them are pitched toward the under-twenty-five crowd. Youth has been labeled a $38 billion market. That means that most young people have money — for the same purposes that adults have money — to spend on products, services and entertainments.

If your parents don't supply an adequate amount of cash, you have to look elsewhere to secure additional dollars. And as soon as you do this, you're caught with the problem of what money is all about. What does it really mean to earn and spend it? How should it be earned? How should it be spent? Does money have any significant meaning beyond earning and spending? Could we get along without money as some young people suggest? Is it an absolute necessity in society, regardless of the form of government in the society?

Let's first establish why we use money. Simply put, money is a means of exchange. We provide a service or make a product for another person and he or she pays us what that service or product is worth to him. We give a certain portion of our time and talent to someone else. We trade a portion of our life for something of theirs. The recipient of our contribution can either give us an equal amount of his time and talent or do it in the commonly accepted fashion of society — give us money. This, in fact, is a more simplified way because we might not need a similar service performed nor might we be able to calculate the actual effort and talent put into a specific act so we could return an equal amount.

Let's take an example: A city dweller needs food. He goes to a farmer. The farmer says, "Drive my tractor for three hours and I'll give you a sack of potatoes." So far it sounds good — except you don't know how to drive a tractor! Besides, he could never come to your city lot and perform a tractor-driving service for you. So you use the accepted means of exchange. You give him $7.50 for the sack of potatoes.

It doesn't make too much difference whether the head of government is a president elected by the people, a prime minister selected by a parliament, or a dictator who ruthlessly grabbed control, money is still essential to exchange one's time and talent for another's goods and services. The only significant factor in the type of government under which you live is that in a democracy you, rather than the government, decide how you want to earn and spend your money — and to a large degree, how much you want to earn and spend.

Everyone soon learns that money means power. You get service in a restaurant because you can pay for it. You purchase an automobile, fine clothing, entertainment — all with money. Your money controls what others do for you and supply to you.

By offering money you can persuade people to cooperate in keeping you warm, supplying your food, making you healthy, stylish and respected. What could be more efficient than using money to do all this? By the appropriate disbursement of money you can please your parents, entertain your friends, and even secure the gratitude of the needy. It's not much different from the viewpoint of industry or government. Money means power. Money means added production. Money means the purchasing of products and resources and the selection of services offered by individuals.

Everywhere you turn, it's a monetary society. And though it would be foolish to assume that money can solve every problem in society, money is still necessary to solve many problems. Many problems in our society would be solved more quickly simply by a wiser use of money.

After saying all this, we ask, Is money bad? Why did Jesus warn men about their relationship to money? Why did Jesus say that a rich man (and in comparison to those to whom He had reference, most Americans would be classified as rich) would have difficulty entering the kingdom? (Matt. 19:24).

Martin Luther came up with an enduring answer when he explained the tenth commandment: "What is it to have a god? What is a god? A god is that to which we look for all good and in which we find refuge in every time of need. Many a person thinks he has God and everything he needs when he has money and prosperity; in them he trusts and of them he boasts so stubbornly and securely that he cares for no one."

The biggest problem we have with money probably isn't the desire to have it, or even the number of things we can purchase with it. Our problem is that we get the idea money can make us free. We feel we can purchase any type of life we desire, ignoring the fact that money can easily enslave us and can become our god!

Jesus said to the rich man, "Get rid of all your wealth and follow Me." In that moment the rich young man sorrowfully discovered his god — he had become a slave to his money. Jesus taught that possessions often possess the possessor. Money can become a major threat to faith; it can destroy one's faith in God, one's love for his neighbors, one's sense of values. Thus Jesus made it clear that, "No servant can be slave of two masters; for either he will hate the first and love the second, or he will be devoted to the first and think nothing of the second. You cannot serve God and Money" (Matt. 6:24, NEB).

Whatever a person comes to love, trust and

fear above all things is really his god. Money or wealth is an inadequate god because it can so easily be lost or change in value. Though some people dedicate their lives to becoming rich, sooner or later they discover that wealth disappoints them. The money-worshiping man is often anxious and insecure. He worries whether he'll be able to gain more or lose all! He finds it difficult to maintain wholesome attitudes toward others. Money-addiction often robs a person of his capacity to love. Loving money gets in the way of loving people.

You say, "This will never happen to me. Our generation isn't hung up on money." You can't be too sure. As a Christian, are you developing attitudes that will shift your thinking away from getting and spending money on yourself and toward what it can do for others? You'll have to begin right now if you are going to avoid a selfish attitude toward money. Now is the time to discover the biblical principles of stewardship. (Read Luke 16:1-13 and Matt. 25:14-30).

Maybe God is calling you to lift the burdens of poor people throughout the world. Maybe God wants you to help change the hang-ups Christians have about gaining and spending money. Perhaps God wants you to help people see that money can be a tool to accomplish worthy goals rather than just a means to fulfill selfish desires. If you are not hung up on money yourself, then you will place a high priority on using some of your personal money to benefit others. You can demonstrate the best use of money now even though you may have very little.

Perhaps churches have spent too much money on buildings in the past. What can Christian young people do to see that this mistake isn't repeated? Perhaps the older generation puts too much value on the symbols of prosperity. What can Christian youth do to assure that material things do not continue to dominate our thinking?

WHAT DOES THE BIBLE SAY?

"People prepare a banquet for enjoyment and wine cheers the living; but money has to bring about everything" (Eccles. 10:19).

"But Peter answered him: 'May you and your money go to hell, for thinking that you can buy God's gift with money" (Acts 8:20).

" 'Then I will say to myself: Lucky man! You have all the good things you need for many years. Take life easy, eat, drink, and enjoy yourself!' But God said to him, 'You fool! This very night you will have to give up your life; then who will get all these things you have kept for yourself?' And Jesus concluded, 'This is how it is with those who pile up riches for themselves but are not rich in God's sight' " (Luke 12:19-21).

"The wealth of the rich man is his fortress; the ruin of the poor is their poverty" (Prov. 10:15).

"He whose eye is evil hastens after wealth,

but he does not know that want will come upon him" (Prov. 28:22).

"Do not save riches here on earth where moths and rust destroy, and robbers break in and steal. Instead, save riches in heaven, where moths and rust cannot destroy, and robbers cannot break in and steal. For your heart will always be where your riches are" (Matt. 6:19-20).

"Jesus then said to his disciples, 'It will be very hard, I tell you, for a rich man to enter the Kingdom of heaven. I tell you something else: it is much harder for a rich man to enter the Kingdom of God than for a camel to go through the eye of a needle'" (Matt. 19:23-24).

"No servant can be the slave to two masters: he will hate one and love the other; he will be loyal to one and despise the other. You cannot serve both God and money" (Luke 16:13).

"Command those who are rich in the things of this life not to be proud, and to place their hope, not on such an uncertain thing as riches, but on God, who generously gives us everything for us to enjoy. Command them to do good, to be rich in good works, to be generous and ready to share with others. In this way they will store up for themselves a treasure which will be a solid foundation for the future. And then they will be able to win the life which is true life" (I Tim. 6:17-19).

WHAT DO YOU SAY?

1. Why do many young people reject the money standards of their parents? What standards do they substitute?

2. How does one establish a Christian attitude toward money? What is a Christian standard of living?

3. In what ways can Christians use their money to glorify God? Is there a universal principle that dictates how every Christian should use his money?

4. What should be the Christian's attitude toward saving and investing money? Toward insurance policies? Toward owning property? Toward retirement plans? Do any of these practices indicate a lack of trust in God? Explain.

5. What portion of the money we earn can we rightfully keep for ourselves? Should tithing be the minimum amount of one's benevolent giving? Should all Christians tithe?

6. When does the pursuit of money become idolatrous? When is it wise to earn as much money as possible? Can a person be extremely rich without loving money?

7. In the Book of Acts, Christians held everything in common. Why did their communal living fail? Is this a sound economic policy for today? What are the dangers? What are the advantages?

8. When the Bible talks about forsaking all to follow Christ, does this mean becoming poor?

Does the Bible teach that we ought to remain poor to maintain spirituality?

9. What are some wrong ways to amass money? Why is money received in an unworthy manner unacceptable to Christians?

Isn't Anything Obscene Anymore? 9

EVERY YOUNG PERSON in high school is familiar with obscene graffiti written on washroom walls. We have become accustomed to seeing obscene words scribbled on public buildings and underground passageways in public parks. However, obscenity is no longer limited to washrooms and tunnels; our society is experiencing a new attitude toward freedom that tends to permit almost any word or action. Four letter words, nudity, homosexuality, erotic films — all are vying for public acceptance.

Pornography has become a word to describe just another form of literature. The sex act is described freely in books and magazines, and obscene language is common on the theater stage and in movies. Words and acts that do not shock your sensitivity are considered dull and unsaleable. What was once spoken and practiced in secret is now blazed across the public media without blinking an eye.

There is a great amount of profit in pornography. Shrewd businessmen are producing millions of dollars worth of films and magazines — erotica of all sorts that is distributed throughout the United States. The American public, which is hardly puritanical, seems to be enjoying this stuff with reckless abandon. It is estimated that the pornography business grosses $1 billion yearly, and it produces highly excessive profits.

Even though many respectable people are disturbed about the increased availability of pornography and obscenity, there seems to be little that can be done to stop it. Community standards no longer serve as moral guidelines that can be used to enforce laws against obscenity. Our highest courts have failed to spell out precise definitions of obscenity and pornography and attempts to enforce adequate legislation suffer from such a handicap. Many argue that it is a constitutional right to produce and read pornographic literature and that no laws should discriminate against it. As a result, hard-core pornography is sweeping the country, bringing immense profits to its distributors, while the average citizen, who is disturbed about it, can do little to change the situation.

Some people fear that laws against pornography would also suppress good literature. Who would be the judge of what is obscene? What might be pornographic to one person may not be to another. Our pluralistic society makes it impossible to agree on these matters, and who really knows what are the true values of society? One lawyer put it frankly ". . . There is no such thing as 'obscenity.' The First Amendment protects all speech and printed matter and the government has no legitimate interest in stifling or limiting the dissemination of communicative material on the ground of obscenity." Another lawyer said, "I would of course define obscenity in terms of the dictionary . . . something that is publicly held to be filthy. But as far as what should be held to be legally obscene I would say there's no such thing and there is nothing that should be legally obscene. . . . The law, basically, is for the purpose of prohibiting conduct which actually and physically hurts other people. And so-called obscene material doesn't really harm anyone."

One of the most explosive reports ever released by a presidential commission was made public in September 1970. The Commission on Obscenity and Pornography, which began its work in 1967, caused a major furor when it made its "findings" public. The commission thought that government should not interfere with the freedom of adults to read or view whatever material they wish. According to the commission, their investigations did not produce any evidence to show that exposure to or use of explicit sexual materials played a significant role in causing crime, delinquency, or sexual deviation. Crime and delinquency were linked with other factors such as bad family relationships and unfavorable peer influence, but exposure to sexually explicit material was not considered an influence on deviant behavior.

According to the commission, the legal prohibitions against pornography have not protected young people from coming in contact with such material. Adults seem to seek such material as a source of entertainment and, for many, pornography becomes a source of information about sex. The commission reported that American public opinion seemed to favor the dissemination of obscene material and said that the public should get what it wants.

The commission advocated that government not be concerned about public morality. Morals should be influenced by the home and religious training and by one's own personal resolutions. Government regulation tends to deprive the person of making a responsible choice on his own, therefore regulations by the government are not desirable.

The minority report of the commission charged that the report did not come to grips with the basic issue, which, to them, concerned itself with whether and to what extent society may establish and maintain certain moral standards. If society is concerned that moral standards be maintained, then it seems logical and legitimate that government at least attempt to protect those standards against forces that threaten them. Public morality, respect for human growth, and respect for family love are strong standards deeply rooted in our culture. The minority members of the commission found it difficult to see how children could grow in love if they grew up with their minds filled with pornography. Pornography is a loveless, degrading influence on a child and reduces man to the level of an animal. According to the minority report, the American public favors stricter laws on pornography. A Gallup poll indicated that eighty-five out of one hundred adults favored stricter laws.

People who produce pornography like to talk about the effects of legalizing pornography in Denmark. They point out that legalization did not have bad effects on people's morals in Denmark and since 1967, when pornography was legalized, convictions for sex offenses dropped rather than increased (this may be due to limited reporting inspired by softer restrictions). Many claim that a wider use of pornography tended to relax the passions rather than stimulate uncontrolled impulses. Some have claimed that the new sexual freedom has actually inspired some marriages which were a little "tired." Others however, have found that obsession with sexual stimuli tended to produce a boredom that killed true sexuality. Pornographic movies were described as "loveless, and even passionless. They are really horror movies, repellent not so much for their immorality as for their inhumanity."

Christian young people should be concerned about the problem of pornography because they are aware of the effects of pornography on people's attitudes and actions. Current society seems to say that pornography is okay for adults, but not for children. Young people are caught in between. Films labeled "adults only" and X-rated movies are considered acceptable for adults, but not suitable for young people under eighteen. The regulation is not based on whether something is right or wrong, but whether or not the audience can take it. The restrictions placed on adult movies are not based upon the rightness or wrongness of what is portrayed, but upon some nebulous concept of "maturity." Christians would argue that wrong is wrong no matter how old you are.

Perhaps the crude enjoyment many adults

receive from viewing pornographic films is the greatest evidence that maturity is not a valid criteria for rating films. The movie industry's ratings are questionable guidelines, for even R- and GP-rated movies often contain what might be considered obscene material by Christian standards. The Christian sees a horrible inconsistency in the values that the world places on "sexual honesty," and "freedom."

Many Americans and maybe some Christians have the idea that if you bring everything out into the open, that somehow makes it all right. They suggest that if feelings of guilt develop by getting your kicks in secret or by sneaking girlie magazines, then it is wrong. To them the sin is not enjoying pornography so much as feeling ashamed about enjoying it. They think that the way to solve the problem of guilt is to bring pornography into the open — this somehow purifies it all.

Christian young people should be aware that present trends toward moral laxity and looser laws will make it easier for the peddlers of obscene material to make it available to more and more people, including young people and even children. Young people are going to have to face inevitable trends toward more explicitness in films, more freedom in magazines, and more perverted sex on television. What will your reaction be? Will you simply become hardened to it and acquiesce to the standards of society? Will you refrain from protest for fear you might be considered a prude? Are you going to permit yourself to become inundated by portrayals of life that are alien to

your Christian conscience and morality? Or
will you delude yourself into believing that once
you are an adult you will be able to handle
sexual deviation portrayed before your eyes
without ill effects?

WHAT DOES THE BIBLE SAY?

"For from the inside, from a man's heart,
come the evil ideas which lead him to do
immoral things, to rob, kill, commit adultery, covet, and do all sorts of evil things;
deceit, indecency, jealousy, slander, pride,
and folly — all these evil things come from
inside a man and make him unclean" (Mark
7:21-23).

"They say they are wise, but they are fools;
instead of worshiping the immortal God,
they worship images made to look like
mortal man or birds or animals or reptiles.
Because men are such fools, God has given
them over to do the filthy things their
hearts desire, and they do shameful things
with each other. They exchange the truth
about God for a lie; they worship and
serve what God has created instead of the
Creator himself, who is to be praised for
ever! Amen. Because of what men do,
God has given them over to shameful passions. Even the women pervert the natural
use of their sex by unnatural acts. In the
same way the men give up natural sexual
relations with women and burn with pas-
sion for each other. Men do shameful
things with each other, and as a result they

receive in themselves the punishment they deserve for their wrongdoing" (Rom. 1:22-27).

"You may be sure of this: no man who is immoral, indecent, or greedy (for greediness is a form of idol worship) will ever receive a share in the Kingdom of Christ and of God" (Eph. 5:5).

"But now I tell you: anyone who looks at a woman and wants to possess her is guilty of committing adultery with her in his heart. So if your right eye causes you to sin, take it out and throw it away! It is much better for you to lose a part of your body than to have your whole body thrown into hell" (Matt. 5:28-29).

"Happy are the pure in heart: they will see God" (Matt. 5:8).

"The eyes are like a lamp for the body: if your eyes are clear, your whole body will be full of light; but if your eyes are bad, your body will be in darkness. So if the light in you turns out to be darkness, how terribly dark it will be!" (Matt. 6:22-23).

"In conclusion, my brothers, fill your minds with those things that are good and deserve praise: things that are true, noble, right, pure, lovely, and honorable" (Phil. 4:8).

"Since you are God's people, it is not right that any questions of immorality, or indecency, or greed should even be mentioned among you. Nor is it fitting for you to use obscene, foolish, or dirty words. Rather you should give thanks to God" (Eph. 5:3-4).

"As for these little ones who believe in me — it would be better for a man to have a large millstone tied around his neck and be drowned in the deep sea, than for him to cause one of them to turn away from me. How terrible for the world that there are things that make people turn away! Such things will always happen — but how terrible for the one who causes them!" (Matt. 18:6-7).

WHAT DO YOU SAY?

1. How do you tell whether something is obscene or pornographic? What standards do you use? What is the difference between pornography and honest art forms?

2. What makes pornography so appealing? Is it normal for young people to be curious about it?

3. The Commission on Pornography claimed that there was little or no relation between pornography and deviant sexual behavior. Do you believe this claim? Why or why not?

4. What makes something obscene? Is it necessary to use four letter words in literature and in movies in order to be realistic? We hear dirty words every day at school and work; is it wrong to use them in movies and on TV?

5. What is the difference between observing a nude painting in an art gallery and seeing nudity in a movie or magazine? Is all nudity

obscene? How do you determine when it is obscene?

6. Why should Christians fight against pornography and obscenity? List some biblical reasons. How should the Christian's opposition to pornography be conducted?

7. Should pornographic material be available to adults or should there be legal sanctions against it? Why?

8. Does free speech mean we can say whatever we please in or out of print? Would obscenity laws contradict the right of free speech?

9. Would governmental regulations of moral choice deprive the individual of the responsibility for personal decision and the formation of genuine moral standards?

10. Who sets "community standards"? Why are such standards a poor basis for determining what is pornographic?

11. What are the best defenses against pornography and obscenity? What can parents do to protect their children from pornography? How should they prepare them for inevitable contact with it?

Why Do Christians Oppose Drinking? 10

YOUNG PEOPLE ARE CONCERNED about traditional values because often their culture is at odds with what they have been taught in their churches and in their homes. Some young people mock the double standards of adults who vehemently oppose drugs that are taken by youth, but who themselves tolerate alcohol and the excesses it leads to. If adults can indulge in drinking hard liquor and risk known mental and physical effects, what harm is there in young people using drugs such as marijuana, which some believe does not produce significant medical or psychological harm? It's easy to show statistics that point out that drunkenness and alcoholism kill more people on the highways alone than drugs do under all circumstances.

Christian young people are concerned about drinking because it is a constant temptation and a growing problem. Like others, Christian young people find that group pressures to drink are as strong as the pressures to smoke or take drugs. Some people feel that taking an innocent social drink has little effect on a person's mental faculties and can do little or no harm. They believe it is possible to drink in moderation without damaging either their body or their Christian witness. They point out that the Scriptures speak of God's provision of all things for man's enjoyment and good. Some quote Psalm 104:14-15, which says, "He causes the grass to spring up for the cattle, fruits and vegetables for man to cultivate, that he may derive sustenance from the land, wine to elate the spirit of man, oil to brighten his facial appearance, and bread to improve a man's health." Those who teach moderation in the use of alcoholic beverages quote I Timothy 4:4, "For everything which God created is good and nothing to be rejected when it is gratefully received" (New Berkeley Version). They point out that Jesus turned water into real wine at Cana (John 2:1-10) and drank wine Himself (Luke 7:33-34).

Jesus used wine when instituting the Lord's Supper (Mark 14:23-25). The apostle Paul advocated wine as a medicine for Timothy's stomach problems (I Tim. 5:23). Some suggest that Timothy's "total abstinence" from wine was the possible source of his stomach troubles. Perhaps drinking unpurified water, without the alcohol in wine to kill bacteria, was a bad practice for Timothy. Those who teach moderation also point out that while the Bible condemns drunkenness and excessive drinking (Prov. 20:1; 23:29-35; Isa. 28:1, 7; Hab. 2:5), it does not command *total* abstinence.

Total abstainers believe that the use of alcohol can lead to evil practices and to the disease of alcoholism. The Christian should abstain from all appearances of evil and deny himself even what might be permissible (I Cor. 6:12).

Total abstinence from alcoholic beverages is considered a challenge to a disciplined life in Christ. It is a matter of conscience and Christian responsibility based on love for God and Christian concern for others. Such Christians do not base abstinence on scriptural practices or precepts but on biblical principles.

The basic biblical principle is: "Are you not aware that your bodies are members of Christ . . . . Or do you not know that your body is a temple of the Holy Spirit within you, whom you have from God and that you do not belong to yourselves?" (I Cor. 6:15, 19). Though these texts in themselves do not require total abstinence, the question remains: Does the consumption of alcohol dishonor the body?

The weak point in the argument for moderate use of alcohol is the difficulty of defining what "moderate use" is. Who is the judge? In our highly mechanized society, the consequences of even slightly impaired judgment are so drastic that it would seem wise to refrain from drinking alcoholic beverages in any amount. By so doing, a person never runs the risk inherent in "moderate" use — using alcohol in excess in convivial circumstances, or as a method of escape from difficult problems.

Another biblical principle that favors abstinence is the principle of concern for the weaker brother. The classic passage is in Romans 14. "One man's faith allows him to eat anything, but the man who is weak in the faith eats only vegetables. The man who will eat anything is not to despise the man who doesn't; while the one who eats only vegetables is not to pass judgment on the one who eats anything, for God has accepted him. . . . So then, let us stop judging one another. Instead, this is what you should decide: not to do anything that would make your brother stumble, or fall into sin. My union with the Lord Jesus makes me know for certain that nothing is unclean of itself; but if a man believes that something is unclean, then it becomes unclean for him. . . . Do not, because of food, destroy what God has done. All foods may be eaten, but it is wrong to eat anything that will cause someone else to fall into sin. The right thing to do is to keep from eating meat, drinking wine, or doing anything else that will make your brother fall" (Rom. 14:2-3, 13-14, 20-21).

When Christians set such an example they establish a social climate in which abstinence becomes accepted behavior. By setting an atmosphere for society, the church provides an insurance against intemperance. This is not to suggest anything like the Prohibition Amendment which turned out to be a complete failure. It is not a question of forcing others *not* to drink, but as Christians, showing such a concern for Christ, for our bodies, for our fellowmen and for the good of society that we refrain from that which is potentially a tragic evil.

There are approximately seven million alcoholics in the United States. This figure increases at about four hundred thousand a year. Alcoholism is the nation's third most serious health problem and costs Americans billions of dollars. Drinking causes over twenty-five thousand automobile deaths a year; this is almost half of all auto deaths. There is no question, then, that drinking is a moral problem to be faced by Christians.

The medical profession and psychological researchers have devoted much time to the causes and cures of alcoholism. However, there is no secret about the surest way of preventing it. *He who never takes a drink will never become an alcoholic.* The Christian does not look upon drinking in terms of his own pleasure, or even in terms of the "innocent" social drink, but in terms of the consequences of such a practice upon himself, upon other individuals and upon society.

Christians must admit that abstinence makes sense regardless of differing opinions, traditions and interpretations of what Scripture says about drinking. Today's young people, who are the potential drinkers of the future, must evaluate the case for abstinence, whether or not it is a valid and acceptable approach to drinking.

It would not be fair for young people not to be fully informed on the hazard of alcoholic consumption. Once a young person recognizes the dangers, to indulge in or refrain from drinking boils down to a personal decision and commitment to God. Paul's principle was one of restricting his liberty out of consideration for the weaker brother. He said, "Everything is permitted me, but not everything is beneficial. Although everything is allowed me, I will not be mastered by anything" (I Cor. 6:12, New Berkeley Version). "Everything is allowed, but not everything is helpful. Everything is allowed, but not everything is constructive. Let none seek his own advantage, but rather that of his neighbor" (I Cor. 10:23, 24, NBV). "It is well to eat no meat and drink no wine, to do nothing that would make your brother stumble" (Rom. 14:21, NBV).

Young people who are not hooked on alcohol or drugs, should see that abstinence from either of these dangerous chemicals can be only on a voluntary basis. Group enforcement has always failed. For the Christian, it is a personal commitment. To refrain from drinking, which has so many dangers, benefits not only the individual, but also others who will be influenced by your habits and life style. The Christian young person who is sensitive about his Christian witness will find it a small denial to abstain from drinking.

WHAT DOES THE BIBLE SAY?

> "He causes the grass to spring up for the cattle, fruits and vegetables for man to cultivate, that he may derive sustenance from the land, wine to elate the spirit of man, oil to brighten his facial appearance, and bread to improve a man's health" (Ps. 104:14-15).

> "John the Baptist came, and he fasted and drank no wine, and you said, 'He is a madman!' The Son of Man came, and he ate and drank, and you said, 'Look at this man! He is a glutton and a wine-drinker, and is a friend of tax collectors and outcasts!'" (Luke 7:33-34).

"Do not drink water only, but take a little wine to help your digestion, since you are sick so often" (I Tim. 5:23).

"Watch yourselves! Don't let yourselves become occupied with too much feasting and strong drink, and the worries of life, or that Day may come on you and suddenly" (Luke 21:34).

"Let us conduct ourselves properly, as people who live in the light of day; no orgies or drunkenness, no immorality or indecency, no fighting or jealousy" (Rom. 13:13).

"Do not, because of food, destroy what God has done. All foods may be eaten, but it is wrong to eat anything that will cause someone else to fall into sin. The right thing to do is to keep from eating meat, drinking wine, or doing anything else that will make your brother fall" (Rom. 14:20-21).

"Someone will say, 'I am allowed to do anything.' Yes; but not everything is good for you. I could say, 'I am allowed to do anything'; but I am not going to let anything make a slave of me. You know that your bodies are parts of the body of Christ. Shall I take part of Christ's body and make it part of the body of a prostitute? Impossible! Don't you know that your body is the temple of the Holy Spirit, who lives in you, the Spirit given you by God? You do not belong to yourselves but to God; he bought you for a price. So use your bodies for God's glory" (I Cor. 6:12, 15, 19-20).

"A church leader must be a man without fault; he must have only one wife, be sober, self-controlled, and orderly; he must welcome strangers in his home; he must be able to teach; he must not be a drunkard or a violent man, but gentle and peaceful; he must not love money; . . . Church helpers must also be of a good character and sincere; they must not drink too much wine or be greedy" (I Tim. 3:2-3, 8).

(See also: Titus 2:3; I Cor. 11:21; John 2: 1-12)

WHAT DO YOU SAY?

1. How does alcohol work in the body? What are the dangers of drinking alcoholic beverages?

2. In the light of biblical practices and present day attitudes toward drinking, is moderation still a valid approach for Christians? If so, what justifies it?

3. What is moderate drinking? How much is moderate? What are the weaknesses of the moderation approach?

4. Should Christians avoid drinking moderately only because there are risks involved?

5. Are the dangers of drinking alcohol adequate reasons to favor abstinence? What reasons beside risks can be used to support abstinence? What biblical principles support the idea of abstinence?

6. Can a total abstainer be a better witness

for Christ than a person who drinks moderately? Are there ways in which a moderate drinker can be a better witness? Is it okay to drink in private as long as you won't hurt anyone?

7. Is the concept that alcoholism is a disease in harmony with Scripture? Does this concept dilute the idea that excessive drinking is sin? When does drinking lead to alcoholism?

8. Do you think Christians should use wine or other liquor in cooking? Should a total abstainer refuse to eat something that has been cooked in wine? What was the apostle Paul's principle?

9. Does the idea of total abstinence deny the biblical affirmation that all God's creation is good and therefore to be enjoyed in moderation by man? Isn't excess of any kind a sin?

10. If moderation is the practice of most Christians in relation to most things — eating, exercise, material possessions — why is alcohol singled out for abstinence?

11. What is the best way to refuse an alcoholic drink when one is offered at a party or at a friend's home? Do you have to feel embarrassed about it?

12. How can Christian young people meet the pressure to drink with friends? What Scripture or biblical principles should be remembered when faced with this temptation?

13. How does one's relation to Jesus Christ affect one's attitude toward social drinking? Is a person who abstains from drinking more "spiritually minded" than one who drinks moderately?

Can We Talk to the Dead? 11

WE ARE WITNESSING many strange practices in the world of youth as they seek to find meaning for life: the performance of marriages in the name of Satan, worshiping Satan in place of God, attendance at seances with mediums who claim to talk to deceased relatives (of those who pay the fee), drug-incited "religious" experiences in which users claim to go beyond death — where time seems no more and where the user communicates with spirits and "sees" God.

Are there such things as demons who perform some of these activities? Do people really talk to the dead? Do mediums receive messages from the world beyond? Is Satan-worship real, or a publicity hoax?

With movies and books portraying the bizarre in so many forms, with many new cults coming into prominence, and with young people searching for more than what the established church has offered, it is not strange that young people get entangled in psychic and spiritual phenomena. Bizarre spiritual happenings present an intriguing field for investigation and a Christian young person has to ask himself, How much may I get involved? Is it permitted to visit mediums who claim to communicate with the dead? Do demons control people as in Bible times? Are occult practices blasphemous?

A Christian's interest in spiritism stems from the prohibitions given in the Bible against consulting mediums and wizards, and from questions about the reality of the spiritual world. While Christians do not condone the practice of consulting mediums, they are interested in supernatural phenomena as they relate to questions about the "other world" and life after death — doctrines often denied by modern scientific men.

Scientists have done a considerable amount of investigation into the work of mediums, seeking to discover what, if any, supernatural power they possess. The Institute of Parapsychology in Durham, North Carolina, has been studying such things as predicting the future and extrasensory perception (ESP). In over forty years of research, they have shown that some kind of perception does exist beyond the normal senses.

Psychics have become popular for predicting events. Jeanne Dixon, the famous forecaster, predicted the assassination of President Kennedy, the downfall of Premier Malenkov of Russia in 1955, the orbiting of Sputnik in 1957. Of course, a large percentage of mediums and seers are probably nothing more than clever people who, because of a keen sensitivity to human nature, are able to feed on the gullibility of their fellows.

However, enough evidence has been collected to make it logical to recognize ESP and "the gift of prophecy" as realities to reckon with whether demonic or not. Christian honesty demands that such phenomena be taken seriously and evaluated in relationship to what is taught in the Bible. An honest evaluation will help Christian young people avoid three major pitfalls: first, getting involved in practices that seem innocent but intriguing — at the outset; secondly, denying that such things exist, without making a thorough investigation; thirdly, being influenced by people who possess supernatural powers of which the young person is not aware.

Well-known clergyman-psychic Arthur Ford, founder of Spiritual Frontiers Fellowship, claims that psychic experimentation is beneficial even to Christians. He claims his spiritistic powers are a gift from God as described in I Corinthians 12 where Paul lists healings, prophecy and the ability to distinguish between spirits. He says that if your motive is God-centered, you are free to explore anything in the spiritual universe without fear.

Merrill F. Unger, Old Testament scholar and author of the book, *Biblical Demonology*, takes a different view. He says that spiritualism (or spiritism) is dangerous. He identifies it with ancient necromancy — something forbidden by God. Unger points out that although much that passes for present-day spiritism is pure chicanery, nevertheless, real communication with the spirit-world does happen at times. He says that modern spiritism is nothing more than ancient sorcery, with a particular emphasis on communicating with supposed spirits of the dead. Such communication, according to Unger, is a deception performed by impersonating demons. Basically it is demonism. He notes that the word "medium" can be substituted by the words "demonized man" and/or "demonized woman."

The inquisitive Christian young person, who wants to explore psychic phenomena, must ask: At what point am I dealing with legitimate psychic phenomena and at what point will such activity trespass into enemy territory forbidden by God? While recognizing the reality of the unseen world, and the possibility of extrasensory perception, the Christian must beware of becoming too involved and perhaps enamored with such things. One prominent clergyman who claimed to have made contact with the "other side" said, "The demonic is always close — very close!"

From the biblical point of view, it should be clearly stated that deceased people do not come back from the dead to communicate with the living. The Bible teaches that there is a gulf fixed between the living and the dead. No one passes back from the dead to the living. The Bible also teaches that evil spirits impersonate the dead. The only case of a dead person ever returning as a spirit was when God permitted Samuel to speak to King Saul. In that case, it was a glaring exposé of the falsity of spiritism. The medium's terror at the presence of a real spirit stands as good evidence of the fraudulency of her craft.

There's good evidence that the "messages" from so-called spirits are really "lifted" from the latent memories and subconscious feelings of those seeking messages from the departed. This does not deny the powers of demons to control people on earth and to impersonate the departed. But it definitely questions whether contact is actually made with a departed spirit or an evil spirit.

The Christian has no doubts about the spiritual world, whether good or evil. The Bible teaches the reality of both. But the Christian takes seriously the biblical warning not to dabble in contacting departed spirits.

Illustrations, reported from reputable sources, attest to the actual presence and power of demons in our world today.

Evangelical Alliance Mission worker, Arthur Johnston, reports: "I was walking down the Boulevard des Italiens in Paris. I noticed a 25-year-old woman sitting in a chair, blindfolded. She was writing feverishly — giving answers to personal questions viewers asked her about themselves. A man accepted pay for each answer. Later she told license plate numbers of passing cars without hesitation or prompting. Finally a man opened a book and asked her to quote what was on one page. Without seeing the book, she quoted every word of the technical material. I prayed, 'Lord, if this young woman has a supernatural power, in the name of Jesus confuse the spirit.' Immediately after I prayed, the girl became disoriented and unable to continue her spiritistic performance. The crowd noticed her plight and left. I walked away, thanking God for His great power."

Many other illustrations of demonic possession could be cited, but let this be sufficient to support the view that demons are alive and working today. Biblically oriented young people will not be deceived by spiritism and should be a help to those who are. People can be released from demonic practices and false hopes today by the power of Jesus Christ. Even as demons are real today so is the power of Jesus to "cast them out." Young people who are open to the Spirit of God can have this power. Christian young people should be more concerned about "talking" to God than about conversing with spirits and demons.

WHAT DOES THE BIBLE SAY?

"Do not turn to mediums and seek no wizards to defile yourselves by them. I am the Lord your God" (Lev. 19:31).

"There must not be found among you anyone who makes his son or his daughter pass through the fire, anyone practicing divination or soothsaying, observing omens, applying sorcery, a charmer, a medium, a wizard, or a necromancer. For all who do these things are offensive to the Lord" (Deut. 18:10-12).

"So Saul died because of his unfaithfulness in which he acted disloyally against the Lord, because he . . . even tried a medium's seance. He did not look to the Lord, who therefore caused his death and the transference of the kingdom to David the son of Jesse" (I Chron. 10:13-14. See also I Sam. 28:3-25 for the story of Saul's experience with the medium of Endor.).

"For there is one God, and there is one who brings God and men together, the man Christ Jesus, who gave himself to redeem all men" (I Tim. 2:5).

"The Spirit says clearly that some men will abandon the faith in later times; they will obey lying spirits and follow the teachings of demons" (I Tim. 4:1).

"My dear friends: do not believe all who claim to have the Spirit, but test them to find out if the spirit they have comes from God. For many false prophets have gone out everywhere. This is how you will be able to know whether it is God's Spirit: everyone who declares that Jesus Christ became mortal man has the Spirit who comes from God. But anyone who denies this about Jesus does not have the Spirit from God. This spirit is from the Enemy of Christ; you heard that it would come, and now it is here in the world already" (I John 4:1-2).

". . . I do not want you to be partners with demons. You cannot drink from the Lord's cup and also from the cup of demons; you cannot eat at the Lord's table and also at the table of demons" (I Cor. 10:20-21).

"Even Satan can change himself to look like an angel of light!" (II Cor. 11:14).

WHAT DO YOU SAY?

1. Why do many young people take an interest in the spirit world and psychic phenomena? What, if any, are the dangers?

2. How do you explain the prophet Samuel's appearance to King Saul when he consulted the medium of Endor (I Sam. 28:3-25)? What was the nature of that appearance? Did the medium actually cause Samuel's appearance?

3. Why does God forbid consulting mediums and wizards? What motivation in seeking knowledge through a medium is contrary to God's revelation?

4. Is there a relationship between demonic activity, modern spiritism and Satan worship? Explain.

5. Is there a difference between communicating with the spirit world and scientific psychic investigation?

6. How do you react to people who seem to possess a "gift of prophecy"? Should we attribute such a power to God when predictions come to pass? Why or why not?

7. In what ways does present psychic research confirm the Christian claim of a spiritual and supernatural world? How does it confirm life after death?

8. Drug users have proclaimed entrance into a world beyond their present existence and have what they label "spiritual" experiences. How do you explain such experiences? Are they biblically valid? Do you think this might be one form of demon possession?

9. What is the difference between the "gift

of the Spirit" (I Cor. 12:1, 4, 7-11) and the claims of spiritism? What is the biblical test of a true spirit?

10. Should a Christian young person visit services where Satan is worshiped? conduct psychic research? Why or why not?

Is Automation Depersonalizing Us? 12

"NUMBER 7463-335, take your place next to 7463-337. Number 7463-336 has a 216 [common cold] today," screeched out the computerized voice from the loud speaker in the gymnasium. 7463-335 grumbled, "I won't." A highly sensitive hidden microphone picked up his reply, fed it back into the computer. The computer answered in a few seconds, "7463-335, report to detention room 103 immediately after your 1:45 biology class."

A make-believe situation or something from a new edition of Orwell's *1984?* Possibly, but the above situation illustrates one of the greatest fears of modern youth — the fear of depersonalization in the computer age. Youth today look upon the computer as a monster ready to pounce upon the unprotected. Some wonder whether computers will be developed with the ability to think for themselves.

Whether or not that be the case, computerization and automation have made deep inroads into our society. Future technological advances stagger our imaginations.

Computers at work in business calculate complex financial problems, forecast sales, determine the best areas of the country in which to market products, and check anyone's credit rating in a few seconds. The catch, however, is that all information programed into a computer must originate from the creative minds of men. Computers do only what they are told — on the basis of what has been stored in their electronic "brains." They can do no more than this! Computer programmers speak of "garbage in, garbage out."

In the medical field, automation reduces the suffering of thousands of patients; assists doctors in making proper diagnoses and then finds effective treatments based upon previously treated cases in other parts of the country, which in turn speeds up the healing process and saves many patients from death or undue suffering. A doctor can now have a complete print-out of a patient's previous symptoms, treatments, reactions, etc. — all through computer technology.

Modern food processing is becoming more automated. Farming is also an automated industry and farms can produce far greater crop yields with fewer workers. The phenomenal advances in space exploration and flights to the moon would have been totally impossible without accurate and speedy computers. Computers are the heart of the space exploration of the Apollo series and are able to make precise calculations for interpreting and feeding information to electronic equipment that will make the minutest changes to correct a space flight pattern. Some computers are capable of making millions of calculations per second — a feat impossible for men.

Scientists are even talking about the possibility of computers reproducing replicas of themselves. Through the combination of biology and electronics — "bionics" — they say that such feats as reproducing life by computer are possible.

Looming over all the progress achieved by modern technology is the haunting fear that we might create a computer that will eventually take over control of man. Some have asked, Could man create a machine that would control all humans? Once the button is pushed on such a machine, even the button pusher would lose the power to control it and mankind would, for all practical purposes, be controlled by a computer. Man would be the slave of his technology. It sounds fantastic, but some scientists are worried about the possibility because we have seen a staggering amount of science fiction become reality in the past few decades.

Two questions rise in men's minds about the result of our technological revolution: What is man becoming? and, What will become of man?

The first question concerns the influence of modern technology on man psychologically, morally and socially. Is modern man in danger of becoming depersonalized to such a degree that he amounts to nothing more than a controllable robot? Will man become a servant of the very technology he has created? Will the fears, unrest and inevitable change in a highly technological society breed a humanity controlled by pills, the formulas of which were created by a computer? Will a new generation, largely taught by teaching machines rather than by people, shake off all respect for accepted traditional and moral standards? Will despotic control be made easier when men's minds are conditioned by global communication networks?

The second question asks: What will become of man? The question concerns itself with man's future and his existence on this planet. Major world powers now have the ability to destroy one another and most of the rest of the world. All this is possible through man's scientific accomplishments. With no signs that the nations of the world are willing to disarm, this is frightening. The secrets of the atomic and hydrogen bombs are getting into the hands of more and more nations, many of which have the technology to deliver such bombs around the world. What will become of man? Will he reduce his existence to primitive conditions by initiating a major holocaust? Will he threaten his very existence by producing the means of destroying himself, to the point where all the world stands in fear of an indiscriminate push of a button?

No matter which of these two questions we consider, they both point us to significant problems of modern life, the problems of really knowing who we are and what is our destiny. Modern technology forces us to ask in a different sense the question the Psalmist posed: "What is man that thou art mindful of him?" What is man's place in the world? What is his place in history? What is his mission?

No matter how technically oriented our world becomes, there remains one outstanding weakness in technology. It cannot demonstrate the human characteristics of love, compassion, understanding, joy, etc. Technology will never duplicate the fruits of the Spirit as outlined in Galatians 5:22-23. Technology can deliver information, compute and diagnose complex problems, and be an instrument of good to mankind, but it will never respond to a human need apart from its human inventors. Man may become so infatuated with his machines that he becomes like them, but machines will never be able to be human. This is the key to our understanding of technology.

Here's where Christian young people can resist the depersonalization that threatens us, and demonstrate the inner transforming power of a Christian personality.

Rebellion against a technological society is not the answer. The answer is application of genuine characteristics of deeply-rooted Christian personality. In the final analysis, any depersonalization that comes to us as individuals comes because we really don't exert the energy and mental creativity to keep fresh and alive as persons. Technology should always remain the servant of human personality. To keep it in that perspective requires the full creativity of the human mind.

For the Christian, what greater bulwark can there be against depersonalization than the operation of the Holy Spirit? The contrast between God's personal interest as expressed to His children, and the growing depersonalization that men allow is more evident when we look at growing technological advancement and bureaucracy in our society. Nevertheless, every young person can have hope; even though you might become a ten-digit number in a governmental file, you can remain a person — indwelt by the unique Person of the universe — Jesus Christ.

WHAT DOES THE BIBLE SAY?

"The law of the Lord is perfect, restoring the soul; the testimony of the Lord is sure, making wise the simple; the precepts of the Lord are right, rejoicing the heart; the commandment of the Lord is pure, enlightening the eyes; the reverence of the Lord is clean, enduring forever; the judgments of the Lord are true and altogether righteous. More to be desired they are than gold, than much fine gold; sweeter too than honey, and the drippings of the comb. Moreover by them is Thy servant reminded; in keeping them there is great reward" (Ps. 19:7-11).

"See to it, then, that no one makes a captive of you with the worthless deceit of human wisdom, which comes from the teachings handed down by men, and from the ruling spirits of the universe, and not from Christ. For the full content of divine nature lives in Christ, in his humanity, and you have been given full life in union with him" (Col. 2:8-10).

"It is true that we live in the world; but we do not fight from worldly motives. The weapons we use in our fight are not the world's weapons, but God's powerful weapons, with which to destroy strongholds. We destroy false arguments; we pull down every proud obstacle that is raised against the knowledge of God" (II Cor. 10:3-5).

"There is for us only one God, the Father, who is the creator of all things, and for whom we live; and there is only one Lord, Jesus Christ, through whom all things were created, and through whom we live" (I Cor. 8:6).

"Instead, give first place to his Kingdom and to what he requires, and he will provide you with all these other things. So do not worry about tomorrow; it will have enough worries of its own. There is no need to add to the troubles each day brings" (Matt. 6:33, 34).

WHAT DO YOU SAY?

1. In what ways does man lose freedom as technology becomes more of a factor in daily living? Are these losses a detriment to freedom of expression? How do they infringe on Christian liberty?

2. What tendencies develop when men put too much dependence upon electronic technology? Why should these tendencies cause alarm?

3. To what is modern technology leading man? Name the good things as well as the

bad. Do the good ones outweigh the bad? Explain.

4. Young people often deride technological advancement. How can this be harmful? helpful? Why?

5. What attitudes should Christians have toward modern scientific advancement? Toward computerized processes that tend to depersonalize people?

6. Name ways in which you think modern technology has depersonalized you (made you less of a person). Is there too much fear of the depersonalizing process? What creative ways can you suggest to overcome depersonalization?

7. Is there anything in the human personality that will prevent man from becoming a slave to the technology he invents? How do you explain man's willingness to become servant to technology?

8. What can Christian young people do to help their churches develop a spiritual thrust within the technological age?

9. How can Christians help men preserve the attitude that the spirit of man is superior to the technology he devises?

10. How can Christian young people use modern technology to bring others into a personal relationship to Jesus Christ?